THANK YOU, FEAR
I'LL TAKE IT FROM HERE.

DEDICATION

For my younger self. The version that had trouble believing that I am good enough, I am worthy enough, and I am strong enough. You are a survivor, and I am grateful for your strength. Today, *I know* I am good enough, worthy enough and strong enough. Thank you for pushing through.

For the people in my life who have never stopped showing up and loving me through it all, my family, and friends. You have shown me strength when I wasn't sure I had it.

For Meric. I have learned more from you than any other human on this planet. You are wiser than your years and have given me the drive to keep pursuing my dreams. I am in awe of how true you are to yourself and how you show up authentically for others. You are a guide in this world. Keep guiding.

For my husband, Eric. You are my rock. The one who has supported me through my twists and turns, mind changes, mood changes, and personal growth. You have shown me how to use my wings to fly even higher. Your patience and love have given me the space and courage to keep exploring my limitless opportunities.

Thank you, Fear

I'LL TAKE IT FROM HERE.

MANDY GRENIER

Smoky Quartz Press

Thank You, Fear – I'll Take It From Here

Published by Smoky Quartz Press
Francestown, New Hampshire
USA
www.mandygrenier.com
Contact publisher for bulk orders and permission requests.

Interior book design & formatting
by Leesa Ellis of **3 ferns books** ➣➔ **www.3fernsbooks.com**

Printed in the United States of America.

Library of Congress Control Number: 2021917047

ISBN: 978-0-578-96765-3

Table of Contents

Downloadable Workbook

As an added gift to my readers, a free
downloadable workbook that accompanies
Thank You, Fear – I'll Take It From Here
is available at
www.mandygrenier.com/thankyoufear

Introduction

*I*t's 3 am the usual time that I wake up rolling around in my bed because there is so much on my mind. This time it was the constant playback of what the hell am I doing with my life? I am happy, yes, in terms of my family and security – to an extent on the security. I'd like more choices, for sure, but we have a home and we are fed, and we generally are able to have the things we'd like or at least work on attaining them. This 3 am date I have daily though is not about the surface happiness, it's about me! "What the hell are you doing, really?" that's the voice, then I immediately get a feeling of loss, guilt, despair, and surrender. "Well, I'm not fulfilling all of my desires, that's for sure, but we can pay our bills." That is what I say as soon as I start to go down the ugly path of self-pity. It's easy to reassure myself that up until the moment of contemplating my unhappiness, it's not a complete loss. There are many things that I can say are accomplishments and that I am extremely grateful for.

My 3 am freight train of thoughts happened almost every morning for most of my adult life. Sometimes I could fall back asleep, other times I lay awake beating myself up for being such a loser and not having more in my life. I named this my 3 am Monster because I felt if I named it, I could start to control it. Not this monster! It had a tight grip on me and when I started doing some reflection on my monster, I learned that most of this was what I understood to be fear. The fear of not doing what I want in my life, and as I am getting older, having to accept it and embrace this path I have created because let's face it, it's my reality and there is no way out... Cue the record scratch – WHAT? Yes, that is truly what I would say to reduce the fear and continue on living as I had been, day by day, week by week, month by month, year by year.

Honestly, the yearly New Year's resolution was a complete joke. I knew it too as I would say it or write it in my journal. It normally looked like this: This year I am going to finally start my own business, write a book, and upgrade things around my house. Hell, I'd even throw in things like buying a new pair of jeans. I needed one thing that I was truly going to get done, so I could say something happened that fulfilled that stupid resolution.

Then, one day, I said, "Screw this, today is different." It was an early spring morning and spring in New England feels like a rebirth. The snow is melting and the earthy smell starts to emerge. Birds return and greet you in the morning and it feels like a choir is singing from above. Tiny flowers begin to break ground and the earth is damp. There is a feeling attached to spring for me-it's the feeling of new opportunity. This morning at 3 am, I woke up, greeted my monster, but it felt different. Instead of the constant barrage of self-doubt, worthless comments that I normally encountered, I heard, "Just DO something different to change your outcome." Okay, I thought, something different. So, I got out of bed. I went to the living room and started writing down some ideas of what I would like to do with my life, something different.

I sat there for a few minutes, thinking there must be women all over the world that struggle with self-doubt and fear, right? Or am I the only one who allows this shit to stand in the way of everything I REALLY want in life? No, there are others, I'm sure of it.

Here I am, a mom of a teenager, in my late 40's, married to a supportive husband, and I've got nothing figured out? Oh, and I should mention this went on for a long time, so I decided that one thing I could do right away is to release alcohol in my life to help me focus. I did that, and within a month, a pandemic was rolling over our tiny state and the world. What the hell was I thinking, how am I going to weather this storm without a little wine? Holy shit, this clarity I was seeking was about to get squeaky clean, but I didn't know it, not at that moment.

In one year, I quit drinking, finished up my college degree and graduated, started writing this book, began creating an e-course for women who would like to transform their lives by shifting from fear to freedom, enrolled in a certification program to become a professional coach, and watched my son go from middle school to high school. To say a lot happened in a year, would be an understatement. Doing all of this while working at a school full-time during a pandemic has been both difficult and interesting, but it also has been a time of great reflection and growth.

Within the pages of this book, I will share my struggles, stories about my life, what I've learned, and how I've transformed my fear into freedom by trusting myself to know what it is I truly desire. This book is for the woman who knows that there is something more in her, strives for big goals and dreams, but inside hears the voice she thinks she fears. This book is about leaning in, not away, learning what fear really is, how to untangle it, and how to grow with it. It's not about moving through it once, it's about learning how to listen and move with it whenever you want, wherever you want, and however you want.

In this book, you will embark upon a place inside of you that has everlasting beauty and is the valley of your true self. No one else is allowed in there because no one else will ever have the insights, knowledge, experiences, and desires exactly like yours. This is your serene place and only your serene place. It's where your soul runs free and dreams and plays and loves from the highest place of yourself. The thing you call fear, that you were trained to recognize as frightful, is a calling that is being silenced by you. This book will put your ear to the calling and listen with courage so that you can dance freely as the beautiful soul you are in this thing we call "life".

"Change the way you look at things and the things you look at will change."

— Dr. Wayne Dyer

Chapter One

The pain of never fulfilling your deepest desires in life

Back to my 3 am monster

When my 3 am monster wakes me up to remind me of all of my misgivings, slip-ups, missed opportunities, or to let me know I am not living up to much, I usually sit up and decide it's time to move my body in some way to distract the complaints I am hearing. Four years ago when I was greeted by my 3 am monster, I got out of bed, sat at my table and thought, "If I could do anything, (of course I capped it a bit, but I allowed myself to write without judgment), what would I do?" Going back to school was on the list. I started researching colleges. I wondered why this was such a pull for me. See, like many others, I didn't go to college right out of high school, I went to work. I learned a lot, made my own money, and had my own apartment. I tried to go to college and commute daily, but my work schedule and trying to fit into the college social life just didn't work for me. I owe a lot to those days of working hard to survive. Now I can see the skills I gained and how I learned really quickly to adapt to all kinds of situations, but back then the truth is, I struggled, daily.

I grew up fast in our small town and found myself hanging out with kids that were years older than me. Let's just say I experienced things that college kids were just figuring out back in my early years of high school. College social life bored me. I liked the academics but the thought of doing it for four years while commuting and working full time was daunting. I left mid-term. I kept working and climbed my way into some really great jobs. But as I got older, I saw my lack of having a degree as a failure and I assigned it a gremlin that reared its head many times reminding me that I was "not good enough." The constant recording that I heard in my head was, "Why would anyone want to hire you when they could hire someone with a degree?" I wasn't just thinking these thoughts, they were reinforced all around me. Every job listing that appealed to me had a minimum of four-year degree qualification. Every time I applied for jobs I was reminded that I had no education beyond a high school diploma. Years went by and I did okay, but I yearned for more knowledge. I became really good at researching things on the internet, teaching myself, getting really scrappy, but still, I didn't feel I measured up to others who had degrees. I decided to go back to school. The classes I enrolled in were online so I could continue working full-time and help raise our son who was, at the time, just starting middle school. I have a tendency of jumping in whole-heartedly, sometimes taking on way more than others would even think of and pushing myself to my breaking point to prove I am smart enough, strong enough, and basically, just to prove to myself that I am *more* than enough. Obviously, I needed serious convincing. Later in life, I realized how much my perfectionism was standing between me and my dreams. Where did I pick up this perfectionism? I believe it was something I developed over time trying to compete with others in the workplace with degrees, to prove myself and outshine my co-workers. However, it is also the evil voice I hear that reminds me of my failures and holds me in a pattern of doing, and never producing anything.

Searching for answers and looking for direction.

The never-ending swirl of looking for a direction in life looks like this for me and it may look like this for you too – lying awake at night thinking about what I truly want or how I am going to achieve certain goals, often spending too much time just trying to find solutions. Yeah, the solution. What I have found is that I am searching for solutions for things that I am not even sure I want. My direction is scattered and I feel overwhelmed, but I WANT an answer, a direction, a way through however I am feeling. I used to feel that meditation was me lying in a sleeplike state worrying about issues in my life and asking for solutions from someone, somewhere. "Maybe an angel will hear me", I'd say, or "Maybe the universe will provide, or maybe GOD will answer back." Maybe it would sound something like, "I have it all figured out, and here's what you need to do." A magical book would be handed to me, I'd open it, and right there would be the answer, the direction to go in, and a whopping solution to my issue. That is honestly what I wanted, an answer, and most of the time any answer would do. I didn't want to dig deep to actually get to the core of the question or my real feelings, I just wanted a direction.

Over years of doing this, I finally came to the conclusion that I actually do need to dig a little deeper. Okay, a lot deeper. I now understand that getting to the core of my thoughts and feelings offers me the direction that I am looking for. It took time and lots of digging to trust myself. In this book, I intend to offer you some guidance on getting there a little quicker, so you don't have to greet your monster for years and make silly resolutions just to feel as though you attained something this year or that you can attain something at all.

This book will offer assistance but each of us is different in how we process our thoughts and ideas, so be open to digging deeper and asking yourself some hard questions and remember that only you know yourself at this deep level. You will have to dig, ask, and trust yourself to answer honestly and most importantly, love yourself through it. You innately have all the answers inside of you, you just need a little encouragement to allow yourself to use your inner strength and voice to help you answer those hard questions, only you can do this work.

Although I love prayer and meditation and use it daily, nobody understands your true desires better than you. The answers are there, and getting silent and listening is when they will surface. Not by demanding and seeking. Trust me, more struggle and conflict only brings more struggle and conflict. Believe that you have the answers, trust that you are worthy of achieving your deepest most sacred desires in your life because it is possible, more than possible, it is inevitable if you proceed with confidence.

You are a divine being with power beyond what you see and what you experience in your everyday life. This untapped potential inside of you has been waiting for you to greet it in the morning instead of your monster. The lessons in your life that you have learned, sometimes the hard way, are the stone path you will journey down to uncover your greatest strengths. Some lessons you have learned along the path are often more valuable than the answer. Standing on a stone that offers a lesson and reflecting on what you gained from the lesson is some of the most valuable time you will spend on shifting from fear to freedom.

Sometimes while we are out seeking an answer to our question or desire, we end up on another journey and the first question was just a stepping-stone to move you towards another path altogether. When you accept that what lies in the journey is the answer to your desire, you begin to look at yourself and others as limitless beings with a lot of experiences that will never be seen or done the same way. And when we understand that each of us processes, understands, and perceives life experiences differently, we begin to embrace our own story as a unique journey that has no bounds, like a river – sometimes rushing, sometimes trickling, sometimes on its new path seeking the ocean. In that river are the answers and the good stuff that makes you, you. There are no rules as to what you must do to receive anything. All you *need* to do is show up and be willing to allow your river to flow, in any direction, in any manner whether fast or slow because it's all perfect. We never question a tree growing towards the sky to seek nourishment from the sun or the roots that dig deep seeking a drink. However, we question ourselves at every turn at every action as to what this moment will attain for us in the future. We can just be, we can allow the natural unfolding of ourselves, but as humans, we want results now. Society has trained us in this way. We want answers today, this moment. The beauty of the river (your life) is the twists and turns, the widening and narrowing, the rushing and rolling. The destination brings a sense of ending, yet we yearn to discover the destination as though somewhere in the end we get an answer. Why not discover the beauty of the journey our lives take as a river and see what we can find for clues as to our truest, most pure, deepest desires that will help us find self-confidence, self-worth, and clarity along the way?

Learning to trust yourself can seem daunting, downright scary. Remember the game you used to play as a kid when you fall straight back and hope your friend catches you, except she's not there. You fall back and hope *you* catch *you*. It's interesting that we have more confidence in our friends than in ourselves. We do not come into this world believing this, we develop that throughout our lives by messages that we receive. Think back to a time in your life when you had all the confidence in the world and it didn't turn out to be the way you expected. I am having flashbacks to a middle school basketball game. I totally thought I had this shot. I was never a star player on the team, but on this day, I was in the game. I rushed down the court thinking I'd show our coach and the other girls on the team that I could do it! I dribbled, stopped, and took the shot. I was waiting for the cheers and the high-fives. Instead, it went past the hoop and it went out of bounds. No claps just looks and I got a seat on the bench. You see, every time we attempt something new and we fail to reach the desired outcome, we chalk it up to, "I'm not good enough", "I don't deserve a chance", "I am a failure." After years of conditioning ourselves and underscoring these feelings, sometimes loudly, with, "What is wrong with me?", we create the belief that we cannot trust ourselves and that we are not worthy. And in those years, we develop the strong beliefs within us that we are unable to attain the most desired aspects of our lives because we don't deserve it. We don't even trust that we would know what to do with it, anyway, even if we did receive it. That is the place where most of us get hung up in life. Those reinforced words that we take on as our belief system about ourselves then act upon them.

No wonder developing trust in ourselves takes a shit-ton of inner work. We have been telling ourselves for years we are not worthy. Change doesn't come overnight. Change happens when we begin untangling the old beliefs about ourselves and our lives. This is the process in which we take time on each stone in the river to uncover the lessons we learned in life and reflect how it imprinted in our lives and what we decided we were going to hang on to from each experience. Trust in ourselves doesn't always come easy and honestly, I still grapple with it especially when I am doing something new or envisioning a change in my life. However, it is the single most profound act we can do to uncover our deepest thoughts and beliefs and then decide if we want to keep them or let them go. When we try new things, it is natural that we question our ability, so it's quite normal for us to doubt ourselves. The important part is when we do it anyway, when we step in and allow ourselves to try something new and change or challenge an old belief or create a new one, we begin to unravel the old ones and show ourselves that it can be done. When we do that, we rewire self-doubt into self-love and self-confidence. I love Nelson Mandela's quote, "It always seems impossible until it's done." That quote reminds me that as soon as I try something, it's not new anymore. I stop fearing what is going to happen next and can spend my energy crafting the new experience in my way, to bring me joy or decide it's not for me. That's where the good shit starts! Let's get started.

If you struggle with clarity, as I did, and it seems that as soon as you're clear on one thing, you change your mind and begin searching again, you are not alone. Part of this issue is that there are so many choices in our lives, and part of this issue is self-doubt. I personally lived on this wheel for most of my life.

When I am at my height of confusion on what to do in my life I lay in silence, listening to my breathing, allowing a thought or this issue to arise, then I sit with it for a few minutes and see it actually being resolved.

It's a pretty simple process. Here are the steps:

Step 1: Ask yourself, "What did it *feel* like when the issue or task was completed?" Notice to ask **what** it felt like, you're not looking for the answer of *how* it got completed or accomplished.

Step 2: Next, with the feeling of how it felt when it was resolved, name the feeling. Did it make you feel excited, relieved, proud, sad, happy? When you can name the feeling, write it down. The feeling is the emotion that you will focus on to attain the desired outcome.

Here's an example of how this has worked for me. When my son graduated eighth grade, I was struggling with what I should do with my career. I work at a small school and my son was graduating and moving on to high school after being there for ten years. I worked there almost all of those years (nine of them) while he was attending school there. His graduation was a turning point for me, or so I thought. I felt as though it was time for me to move on as well, but I was not sure where or what I wanted to do. I struggled with this for his entire eighth-grade year. Am I leaving, am I staying? Every day it crept into my head and I felt as though I needed clarity around this dilemma. One evening I was lying in bed, exhausted from feeling as though I needed an answer right now. Please finish this agony and let me move in a direction. While I was lying in bed in complete silence, I allowed myself to see the situation as it was and then I went to a place of it being solved, not how, just what I felt when it was solved. I was overjoyed, relieved, excited, happy, thrilled that this would not sit on my shoulders every day. Now, at this moment, I still did not know what I was going to do. I didn't know if I was leaving or staying, but the feeling of knowing it was resolved gave me peace. The next day I went to work and as soon as the feeling of oh no, what am I going to do arose, I went to the memory of me feeling peace and knowing it was all okay. It would resolve itself, by itself. I knew either way if I stay or if I leave, I saw myself in joy. I stayed focused on my daily work and began to enjoy the things I loved so much about my job. The nagging voice asking, "What are you going to do?" silenced enough for my mind to give me the answer. I ended up staying because I sat back and looked around me at all of the joy my job was actually giving me. I love being with children, creating new marketing videos, and posting photos of our kids exploring their learning, and I loved my colleagues. Sure, there are struggles and obstacles in my position and there is always something new happening or we are having to adapt (COVID-19 for example!) but overall, the experience in my position brings me joy. Once I got to the joy, I was able to see it all around me every day, even when I am down, or the gremlin voice kicks in and questions my decision. I can go to joyful moments and place my focus there. This brings us back to the quote at the beginning of this chapter by Dr. Wayne Dyer. "Change the way you look at things and the things you look at will change." It really works. See it in a new light and allow the joy to flow.

Some people do this exercise and see pain when they get to the resolution. That is okay and sometimes part of the process because the issue being dealt with may be causing pain currently and the resolution is more painful due to having to sever a relationship or make a change to bring a resolution. Just know that if you are in this category, it's okay and it's completely understandable to have this feeling arise when you are making a decision to end something that has been in your life or you have a love attachment to it or the person. Take your time, listen deeply to your inner voice, it will guide you and ultimately if you feel pain, it is a signal that a change may be needed to find joy. You are always exactly where you need to be and your inner guidance is your tool for clarity.

Clarity via the Download

I love books, especially audiobooks these days. I listen to them while I am cleaning my house or in my car. I call this my personal and professional development time because let's face it, we are all busy, and squeaking in anytime for ourselves should be celebrated and counted!

When I am struggling with clarity and trying to force my life's purpose onto a piece of paper or have that aha moment, sometimes I feel the need to read every book I can find, because maybe, just maybe that book would spark my intuition to say, "Hey, that's it, that's what you should be doing!" So, I read and listen. It's completely normal for me to have three books going at once. You may also be like that, one for the morning, one for the evening, and one for cleaning or driving time. Or you may be the type that likes just one so you can focus on the content. I sometimes have a short attention span, so like squirrels running, I listen or read for short bursts then jump into tasks or my daily schedule. Some people have the superpower to exercise and listen to books. To all of you, kudos for kicking some ass while devouring a book! I'm working up to that awesomeness. Warning here about reading too many books to find your calling or to help you figure out your life, that can also be a sign of procrastination. We will talk about this in a later chapter.

Usually, when I am reading or listening to books, ideas flow to me and through me. Thoughts stream through my brain and I find myself wandering off into my own realm of creativity. I used to beat myself up for this because I thought I was completely distracted and not paying attention, now I understand that it is just part of the process for me. When you listen or read a book, you pass it through your life filter, all the experiences you have up until this point. It's natural that you'll interpret it in your own way, keeping what works for you, and allowing the words to wander around in your mind, sparking creative thoughts. The good thing about audiobooks is you can pause it and rewind. I cannot tell you how many books I have listened to multiple times. I now embrace this wandering. When you find yourself wandering in a creative space, it is okay to stop reading or listening and write your thoughts down. I have many friends who tell me that they had amazing ideas come to them in the shower or somewhere else where a pen and paper are not readily available. Enter the old-fashioned voice recorder! Not in the shower though! Using your handy dandy smartphone Notes app (there are many voice-to-memo apps out there, I use the Notes app because it's simple, and I like simple) allows you to capture those unfiltered thoughts for later. Those thoughts are gold, they are your stream of unconscious brilliant thinking that is what many people call the "flow". Some call it a download, others call it an inner voice. It's the real deal. It's the true you, channeling your thoughts without analytical smearing and judging. Flow feels so good. Flow allows you to stream your feelings, thoughts, and inner desires. It's like tuning into a radio station inside yourself. I love flow. It lights up my days, nights, drives, dishes, laundry, and someday, yes, running!

Again, flow happens to all of us, therefore, **you are** a creative being with unique thoughts and experiences that are valuable to yourself and others around you. Think of how this world would be without others sharing their creative stream of thoughts with us. Everything that has been created in this world is from one single thought. Someone had an idea or was in the flow and they followed their instinct to bring it to life. You have that power too! We all do. We can think of something and bring it to life. You do not need to be someone else to do this. You need to be you. Kind, open-hearted you. Your thoughts, ideas, and creations matter in this world. We need more people like you bringing them to life, not holding them in. Your uniqueness is your gift to the world, please don't keep it all to yourself. There are people like me, waiting to hear your voice.

Sometimes when we have unique thoughts our inner critic tells us how ridiculous it is and we go back to our old belief system that drags up every missed opportunity or failure (as you perceived it) and then we say, "Yeah, that's probably too hard" or "I'm not worthy of that", so we dismiss it and go back to raking leaves, washing our hair, or driving our car. Hello flow, goodbye great idea, I am not worthy of that desire. That's the typical exchange that happens. But, what if, just for one minute you thought about an idea that you had and then you visualized it actually coming true? What feelings are coming up for you? What emotions do you feel? What if your unique idea feels so far-fetched because you cannot compare it to anyone else's idea, and because we want to validate every thought in our brain, and we can't, we dismiss it? What if the Wright Brothers thought about aviation and said, "Nah, that's never been done, we can't do that, let's just forget about it and go back to cutting the grass." Yeah, that would suck, huh? No planes? I don't know about you but traveling fills me on so many levels. Going to other destinations than where I live, makes my soul sing. I am so glad they had an original idea and went with it!

Here's an example of a flow moment for me. I was driving to work listening to Dr. Wayne Dyer, he's my go-to because his words create a positive synergy in my body. As I turn to make the corner into the driveway of work an idea comes to mind. "I am going to inspire and be inspired by millions of women all over the world because that is my true calling." I know it, I can feel it, I want it more than anything. I want to meet women, I want to hear their stories, I want to share ideas with them, I want to travel around the world. That thought lights me up. I feel energized, excited, I even see faces of women I don't even know yet. I am holding their hands, hugging them, laughing with them, and crying with them. I feel myself now come back into my analytical, judgmental, self-doubting body and hear the words, "Yeah, right, you'll never do that. You are doing what you should be doing and that idea is too big. Make it smaller by A LOT, then let's talk." My amazing tidal wave of good vibes has just been stomped on by the gremlins in my head knocking me down more rungs than I have on my ladder. I can choose at this moment to say, "Yes, gremlins you're right, I am not worthy, nor qualified to inspire anyone" or I can choose to say, "Oh, sorry gremlins I forgot, you like to keep me playing small because the smaller I play, the safer you feel."

When we enter a world of the unknown, our default setting in our brain is to find safety. Safety comes in doing what you always do, nothing more. If you try something new, even tying your sneakers differently (try it) your brain says, "No, we don't do that." Your challenge is to do it anyway. The more you push, even just a tiny bit, the farther the fence gets for the gremlins and the less they complain when you move it little by little. Eventually, your big ideas will become "Maybe's" then "Okay, let's try it!" or, the best one, "We don't have to move the fence that far anymore, let's give it a whirl." We want to protect ourselves from those insecurities we have developed over time by playing small, so we retreat back to old thinking as quickly as we can. Self-preservation mode. How did we get there in the first place? By repetition and determination, both can be great qualities, but like everything in life, good and bad are only labels, what we actually *do* is what sticks.

Connecting action with beliefs.

Everything we do (action) comes from a belief (thought). We are born with zero beliefs, no self-doubt, no self-sabotaging thoughts. We develop them over time from messages we hear around us. Our culture and society play a significant role in forming our beliefs as do family, friends, and the media. Over time the messages we receive become our beliefs and everything that we do is directly related to how we think. If we believe something to be our truth, we act in ways that align with those beliefs. Core values are created as moral compasses by which we overlay our beliefs. You can think of it this way, if you were raised to believe that the sun is a powerful source of energy and your family had solar panels on your home or even valued solar energy, you may have a deep love and concern for the environment as a core value. When you approach a situation in life you will behave based on what you believe and connect them directly to your values. This may influence how you vote, your leisure activities, your lifestyle, etc. If we can trace all of our actions back to our beliefs, then we can begin to understand why we act in ways that we do. If we have two beliefs or values that contradict each other, we find ourselves in mental strain.

When you decide to do something new, you feel this as well. We have been taught to name this feeling "fear". Your entire life when you tried something new and your brain said, "Hold up sunshine, I don't know this and it doesn't align with me", you named it fear and everyone in your life confirmed it. Remember going to school for the first time? Parents, teachers, family members ask if you are scared? We assign the same feeling of being scared with our fears. Or how about riding your bike for the first time? Be careful, you may fall, that will scare you and you won't want to try it again. Why not? Because the power everyone else around you has given to the emotion of how you are feeling. What you were calling fear is actually discomfort in trying something new, that's it! We don't need to give this feeling so much power, but we do.

Fear is a readily available word. Fear has become a powerful and over-used word because any emotion we feel that brings us discomfort, we describe as fear. I'd also like to add that any emotion that gives *others* discomfort can also be projected upon us as fear. Interpreting fear this way is what we are taught and it's easily understood by others. Nobody asks you to explain your fears, they just shake their head and go, "Yeah, I know what you mean." Therefore, we give this uneasy emotion a powerful word that people dislike and try to avoid at all costs. And, we don't even need to explain it, we'd actually rather not and everyone understands why. It's uncomfortable. Our DNA, our instincts, tell us to hate fear. When humans first existed, they feared being eaten by bigger, stronger, animals. We know what it feels like to be afraid of someone or something inflicting harm upon us. We want to erase fear, run from fear, avoid it immediately and forever for good reason. Fear is pain, harm, and threat. It ruins lives, homes, and countries. Fear is encoded in our brain as something to avoid. Period. When we attach discomfort in any form to this word, we give it a strong powerful disliked emotion that we want to avoid.

Now, let's think about trying something new like taking the steps to find a new career that brings you joy. I have met many people who have amazingly beautiful stories about what they see for themselves as the ideal career. When I ask them why they are not presently doing what they describe, most say "fear." "Fear of what?" I ask. Normally, it's fear of not having enough money during the transition, fear of failing, fear of showing up and telling people what they desire in life, fear of sucking at the thing they love, fear of never fulfilling the dream. When I dig a little deeper and ask what it feels like, then it gets interesting. It feels sad, deflating, devastating, embarrassing, exhausting. Okay, now fear has an emotion attached to it. Therefore, it's the emotional pain that is holding them back. All of those feelings are valid and they do exist, and by digging deeper, they can be traced to a belief or block, but true fear is not those feelings. Fear is trying something new and being afraid of danger oh, like skydiving! Yeah, being fearful of the chute not opening. That is fear. Yes, you can argue that the emotional harm technically falls under fear, but I would challenge you to dig deeper. Is it the emotional harm of trying or is it the emotion of falling short of the goal that is tied to a belief or value that we describe as fear? What if we discovered that the true issue is that you have a belief that trying something new should only happen if you are financially stable. Then, if you do not feel financially stable, you are uncomfortable with trying something new. Can that be remedied? Can you find ways to increase your financial stability while trying something new? Does that diminish, even a little bit, of what you perceive as fear? What if you stand on the stone in your river and name the actual belief that is creating the uneasiness with your desired goal and ask if it still serves you? It really is okay to say "No." It is okay to break up with the word "fear."

Beliefs can be changed and so can actions.

Once you realize that your actions come from your beliefs, you may begin to question everything you have learned up until now and how it has affected you along the way. It's completely understandable to begin to pull apart beliefs you've had that you are not sure why or if they even serve you anymore. I remember when I came to this realization, I was sitting in a conference room at a 3-day event in Boston, MA. I looked around the room and wondered if the other 200 attendees were thinking what I was thinking. Can it be this simple? Can I take a long hard look at what my beliefs are and choose to keep the ones that serve me and change the ones that don't to change the trajectory of my life? As heads were nodding at the speaker, the room went completely silent, at least for me, and I sat with the notion that I truly can change what I believe (changing how I am thinking) and in turn, this will change the way I act, see the world, and even better my life's outcome. All of the sudden, the incantation that the group was chanting the day before "I am the creator" took on a whole new meaning. I *actually* am the creator; I decide how my life is going. I have control. Then the real work began.

Feeling lost and overwhelmed because you're so far away from your dream and you're much older now.

Waking up in the morning and rumbling with what the hell am I doing with my life is hard but waking up every morning at 3 am and battling with it, is a soul crusher. Looking back it's hard to even figure out when it first started. I feel that there has always been a part of me that felt left behind, but I never could quite put my finger on what that was. I just knew that no matter what I was doing for work, there was always this nagging feeling like, "Yeah, this is okay, but you're not quite where you want to be, doing what you love." Funny thing is, when I would think about what it is that I love, I would land on adventure, travel, and people. I had a very hard time figuring out how to create a career out of that. I worked in leisure travel for a while thinking that this was the gap I was looking for, but the day-to-day work was not fulfilling. You see, when I said adventure, travel, and people, I meant that I was actually on an adventure, traveling, meeting new people! So, for a great deal of time, I have been looking for that "dream" and telling myself that that is not a "real" job. That is a dream job that is not a part of reality. Plus, you have a family – hello, going on adventures, traveling around the world, meeting new people is not a traditional mom job. Heck, I knew nobody who did that, until I met Mike Dooley!

It was 2013 and I had spent many mornings rolling around in my bed wondering what I was going to do with my life and feeling lost. My current job at the time was okay, but I wasn't going to be in that job forever because I knew I had a nagging feeling that I desired more. One morning while I was reading my *Notes from the Universe*, if you don't get them, they are fun emails that are delivered to your inbox every morning written as the Universe, by Mike Dooley. Anyway, as I was reading that email, I saw that Mike was holding a Train the Trainer event in Boston. I live in New Hampshire, so this was doable for me. I booked my ticket and drove with another attendee from New Hampshire to Boston every day for the three-day conference to learn more. A few months before this conference I was at our local library looking for a good book. I came across Mike's book called *Infinite Possibilities: The Art of Living Your Dreams* and was blown away by some of the content, especially the idea that we create our reality.

That struck me as preposterous and honestly, I had a very hard time wrapping my head around that concept. I wanted to believe it, but it felt so abstract and not something that I had control over. I had control over some things in my life, like how I was scheduling my time, but not the outcome of my life. That is so interesting to me now that I had those thoughts, but at the time, the idea of creating my life was not a reality. Fast forward to the conference.

It's November and I meet the other attendee in a parking lot to ride together, both of us nervous about what to expect, both of us interested in the concept of creating our own outcomes in life. We arrive and register with a group of over-the-top, smiling, bubbly, infectiously positive people outside of the doors (later in life, I actually was in this role!) My first thought was whatever they are doing, I want that! I want to present myself to others in a way that is absolutely infectious with love and positivity, authentically. I received my packet from the registration attendants and we entered the conference room. I found a seat up front. I look around nervously at the other attendees. Some are a mirror of me, cautiously curious, others are dancing on their chairs, some are hugging and laughing. I wait patiently for the speaker to arrive, fidgeting with my notebooks and materials hoping no one would speak to me just in case they asked me about my perspective on life. I didn't quite believe this notion that I am the creator of my life and I didn't want to disappoint them and spoil their first impression of me. Let's face it, I have three days with these people!

After a few speakers, Mike Dooley takes the stage. I am intrigued. What is this man going to say to convince me that I am the creator of my life? It better be good because I am questioning everything that is happening in my life and if I am the answer, then drop it on me because I desire real change, real dream realizations. I have a car that will barely make it to Boston back and forth and if you are saying I can change that, then hell, give it to me. I must admit I was skeptical. Oh my, was I skeptical! I sat with that half-smile, a critic in my head, saying, "Come on, are all these people serious? Do they think we can actually change our lives, ourselves, on our own? Huh, dreamers!"

After a few minutes of his story and his presentation, I was hooked. I felt something changing in me. You know when you meet people who inspire you, open up your way of thinking, and create the opportunity that you are bigger than you perceive? That is what I was feeling. I realized the power within me and the power we all have, every one of us, is readily available at any time. I started to peel back the dark veil that shuttered my desires and started to understand why people were dancing on chairs. The next day we arrived early and again I sat as close to the front as possible. I listened with an open mind and guess what? By lunch, I was dancing on the chairs! No lie, this girl was up dancing on chairs, high-fiving strangers, doing incantations as a group, and believing that I had the power to change my life. You know why? Because I really do have this power, and so do you. We all do. Mike said something though that day that changed my mindset. He said, "Do not worry about the how, just focus on the what." I was stumped for a bit until I listened to his story of knowing he wanted to change his life and he knew he wanted to travel, meet new people, and open his life to adventures. He didn't say or even know how he was going to do it, and little by little he manifested what he has today. He travels the world, going on adventures, meeting new people, and inspiring them to believe in themselves. Hey, that is my dream too! If Mike can do it, so can I, and so can anybody who wants to do it. For me, I had to see someone who actually made this dream happen. I remember looking around the room thinking, these are my people. I have found the people who light me up, who care deeply about themselves and others, and are open to infinite possibilities.

After the conference, I went back to work. Wow, did I ever! My co-workers were wondering what the hell had happened to me. I left on a Thursday full of curiosity, with a bit of skepticism, and returned telling them I never needed to play the lottery again, because I have already hit it big. My life is a gift. I am going to rise to my fullest potential and create my life as I want it. Now, put yourself in their shoes for one moment. They looked at me like someone had sucked my brain out and tapped my ear with a liquid that was infused with a happy gel that unicorns had vomited. I looked like I was planning on taking over a community of followers! They were concerned, no lie. I was getting used to the look though, because my super-supportive husband gave me the same, "Holy shit we lost her" look when I completed my three-day seminar. I was changed. I knew without a doubt that everything I desired was and is inside of me. I have everything I need to become anything I want and guess what that dream of adventure, travel, and meeting new people just became my reality. I was no longer going to settle for maybe, probably not, that's ridiculous, too big of a dream anymore. I had a renewed sense of being. I can now see myself in the role I envision for myself, standing on stages, writing books, and empowering others. I am not Mike, I am me, doing that in my own way. What I needed was the conviction that I can do it, and what I intend to do is get the ball rolling and that is exactly what I am doing and nothing that has happened along the way is an accident. I learned that all I had to do was to trust myself.

Deciding to surrender to your circumstances but feeling a pain deep inside.

When I used to dream about my future and remodeling our house or traveling to faraway destinations, I had a sinking feeling in my gut. A feeling that I instantly knew that what I was thinking was not a reality, it was a dream. Nobody I knew acted on their dreams or at least nobody I knew was bold enough to say, "Hey, this was a far-off dream and I accomplished it" because many people don't want anyone to know their dreams. There is a feeling of shame around dreams. If you say what you really want and it doesn't happen, then you feel as though you failed, you were not meant to achieve this dream. We don't want to be seen as a failure and therefore, we keep our dreams to ourselves and lock them up. The message is do not share your truest desire because it most likely will not happen and you'll look like a failure and worse than that, everyone will know what your truest desire is. Seriously this is what we do as we get older, but not when we are younger. No, when we are younger, adults would ask us all the time, "What do you want to be when you grow up?" children respond with all sorts of things: police officer, firefighter, teacher, veterinarian, hairdresser. But when that one kid says, "I want to be an adventurer and travel the world and meet as many people as possible" then the kind-hearted adults look at each other with that look. You know the one, the oh, how cute, she has a dream look. Very nice, now let's pick something that you may actually do, like become a nurse or a lawyer. We unknowingly suggest to the child, "Hey kid, your dream is unrealistic and it's not going to happen. Pick something that maybe you can achieve." Then, they pick something they wished they achieved and the child has zero connection to their dream. We adapt to others' dreams as if that is the right way of thinking. If it was and is your dream to become a nurse or lawyer, awesome! They may have reinforced that it can actually happen. Usually, it's a different story. Usually, we hear something that we do not have any interest in becoming, but we change our story to fit thiers. We do this for acceptance and belonging.

Our entire life, these messages of our dream being too big, based on other people's opinions that our dream will not happen and we unknowingly accept that. We just add them to a giant piece of baggage that we carry around. Our message bag is filled with these messages that were given to us or that we create. In this case, the child just accepted and stored the message that "Your dreams are too big, too outlandish, too different, get realistic." As we grow, our messages shape our beliefs about ourselves. We accept that we are dreaming too big. We even start to change how we show up. When someone says, "What do you want to do with your life?", we downplay everything as not to create a grandiose idea that others will judge. By experience, we have had our dreams stepped on, so out of protecting ourselves, we say "I'm not sure yet, I am going to stay open to opportunities." Staying open to opportunities is awesome by the way, but in this context, it's a way not to say, "My dream is too big and you'll probably knock it down, so I'll make you feel better by playing small." Think, what is the look you get when you actually put your dream out there? Now, understand that the person giving you the look, got that look too when they were younger all the way up to now. We are trained to pull back, do not share your desire because it probably won't happen. This is why we live small. This is why we do not reach our fullest potential in life and settle for whatever shit rolls down the hill toward us. This is why people are living paycheck to paycheck, underestimating their true value and self-worth. My deepest desire is that something in this book sparks you, just like Mike sparked me so that you can live your fullest life at your highest potential. So that you share it all with the world unapologetically and in all of your glory. The world needs you.

Losing your true identity and placing blame on others for it.

When we are unsure of who we are, we tend to place blame on others because it is easier. We blame our partner for not listening or understanding, we blame our parents for pushing us along in life or not showing up when we needed them, we blame our teachers for lack of direction or misdirection. We blame our doctors, our lawyers, our accountants, we even blame our friends and our children. Blame is shifting responsibility from ourselves to someone else. When we get to the true essence of blame, we discover that there is a lack of something in ourselves that arises. Until we are able to really see what that lack or loss is, we are unable to accept responsibility for our part in it.

Finding the lack or void within ourselves takes patience and real understanding. Not surface stuff. You need to be willing to dig deep. When you find yourself blaming someone else, pause, ask yourself what is the reason for the blame? Do I have a responsibility in this issue? How could I have played a part? When you are truly ready to take responsibility for your part of the issue, you will be open to peeling back the blame and identifying what it truly is that you are blaming others for. Blame does not make the issue go away; it actually intensifies it. If you blame your boss for their lack of involvement in an issue at work, you've stepped over the part where you can step in and resolve the issue at least for yourself. Blame causes more blame, taking responsibility for your part increases the chances of a resolution. We are seeking peace around us and within us. Finding resolution or paths to purposeful action is more conducive to a productive life, than finding someone to shift the blame onto.

When you are struggling with blame, take a deeper look within and ask yourself what your part in the situation is. You may find that you have all of the tools you need to resolve or move the issue further along. We use too much energy on blaming others and not enough on resolutions or finding mutual ownership. Once we can own some of the blame, we can dispel its hold on us and find solutions. Working with others creates tension at times and that is okay.

But blaming others for all of the action or inaction is not production and does not move you forward in your purposeful life. Many times, we blame others to hide our discomfort of stepping up and taking responsibility. We are now in a position to better understand what the discomfort really is, so it's time to see what parts of the situation we can take responsibility for and how we can act to resolve issues.

Feeling overwhelmed by life's demands.

Every day, we all have multiple tasks at hand to get through before we can again feel accomplished enough to lay our head down on the pillow. And even then, there are thoughts, ideas, tasks left undone. We either say, "I can do it tomorrow." or we lay awake beating ourselves up for not making the phone call, paying the bill, setting up a meeting, and so on. The list goes on and on. There is so much happening on any given day in our lives that we start to feel overwhelmed by life's demands or the demands we place on our life.

Have you ever had a day where you have not much to get done? I love those days. I know they are few and far between but let's just go there for a moment. A day where you look at your schedule and think to yourself, "Wow, I don't have anything on my calendar!" Most of us are trained to fill the void. We create tasks and come up with new ones just to keep busy and feel accomplished. Because we know when we lay our head on the pillow, the day will repeat itself and if you did not do much, you'll beat yourself up again just because there were moments of rest. When we have difficulty with rest or allowing our bodies and mind to rest, we actually create more stress on ourselves. We do it because we are trained to fill the void or feel guilt.

We guilt ourselves into believing that if we are not doing something, we are doing nothing. We believe that doing nothing is unproductive and because we do not have much time in our daily lives, moments should be filled. Worse, when we beat ourselves up at night for not doing something we create more of the guilt patterns in our lives and we model this "must be doing" behavior for our children and underscore the belief that if you are at rest, you should feel guilt for it. We create the patterns and beliefs in our own lives and the lives of those around us, especially our children. Why do we feel guilty if we rest? Take some time to go back into your memories and beliefs to uncover what rest means to you. Remember to not judge your responses. They are simply just thoughts that were formed into beliefs over time based on how you were raised and the messages you heard. Why is it difficult to rest? What feelings, emotions, thoughts come up around the word rest or relaxation?

When I sit with the word relaxation, I get a vision of vacation. For me, vacation is a permitted time to relax. Why? I dug deeper and uncovered that, for me, it is what I have absorbed from messages in our Western society. Work hard then you can relax. No rest until you schedule the vacation time and arrive. Then you are permitted to relax. We typically leave our own environment when we vacation, which always makes me wonder about the saying, "It's a great place to vacation, but I wouldn't live here." Why do we save money, block off time on our calendar to go to a place where we permit ourselves to relax, but it's in a place we would never want to live? Interesting.

When I think about our vacations, I think about the beach and palm trees. I think about children laughing and yes, allowing myself to lay around by a pool or the ocean without beating myself up for it. In our Western society, we are programmed to work 40 hours a week (and that is now more like 50-60) for 50 weeks and rest for 2. TWO! What the hell is that message? No wonder we are afraid of sharing our dreams and desires. Most people do not like their job and only get two weeks to rest. Why do we torture ourselves for years, most retire at 65 years old? Why do we save rest for when we are older and do not enjoy life when we are younger? Why is it totally normal to see your family members at gatherings and see how exhausted they are because they have worked 50+ hours weekly to finally have a weekend to relax and when you ask them about what they have been up to, they say "work" with a disgusted look and do not want to talk about it unless they are complaining? Why is this normal? Let's change that, for you and me anyway, and hope it spreads on to our children and generations to follow. One way we can change that is by doing something you love, or at least like, or at the very least, find a way to find joy in what you are doing. There is always something to be joyful about. Again, Dr. Wayne Dyer's quote "Change the way you look at things, and the things you look at change." Find things that do light you up in what you are doing now, then work to create the life you have envisionioned for yourself. If you notice the parts about your work that you do like, and focus your energy on being grateful for those things, more joy will come. Your mindset is what creates the joy around you. Give it a try. Find joy in the things around you and be grateful for those things, even if they are few. Once you begin to change your mindset to find the joy, the joy will follow.

Why most people go through life unfulfilled.

Do you ever wonder if it's easier to surrender to unhappiness or push through the uncertainty of finding happiness? I have. I remember once when I was walking on the beach and this feeling of "Well, at least I have a home, at least I have a car and can feed our family. I should be happy with that and embrace that this is my life." I even remember thinking, "Life is hard, I'm doing okay." I was settling for what I had and what I had was and still is good. And yes, we have a home and a car and food for our family. All those things are wonderful, and I am grateful for that, but something inside was poking up for me saying, "At least? Really?" At least, we use that word a lot. What is at least anyway? At the very minimum, we have these things, and we *should* be happy? Is that how I want to live my life? Is that how you want to live your life? When you look back at your life in your sunset years, do you think you'll be feeling fulfilled? At least, I had a life that I lived, but it could have been better if I pushed past my fears, self-doubt, and worry? Are you okay with living an at least life instead of living a fulfilled, amazing life? Are you okay with living an at least life because we did not want or know how to tame our fears and reclaim our self-doubt and turn them into power? I think not. The time for action is now. No matter where you are in life, change takes action and action can be hard if you are stuck in a lack mindset. Make the real change happen by changing your mindset to abundance and allow abundance and joy to start to change your view on life.

Look around – how many people in your life are truly happy with their work path or life's choices?

Most will tell you they love their family, but past that, it's pretty dismal. Why? Why do we settle? It's easy – that is why. As soon as we begin to see life in a new exciting, challenging yet fulfilling way, our inner self suggests that it's too hard, it's too daunting. You'll look like a fool if you fail, and we shut down. Our inner critic, often called "fear", is using our old brain, the one that was used when our ancestors were outrunning large animals with big teeth to protect them from harm. Our new more advanced brain understands that the reality of a burly large animal with large teeth chasing you because you are stretching beyond your comfort zone is not reality, but the old more primitive brain doesn't know the difference. A threat is a threat even if the threat is getting a new job or starting a workout regime. Your brain doesn't care, all it knows is if we don't do this new thing today, there will be minimal risk, so therefore it's a NO! Stay the same course of action, which is nothing. And, while it's a no, your brain and inner critic decide that hey, she may still be on the fence so let's throw a bunch of mean, destructive words at her and she'll stumble, judge herself and we'll be done. No change, no worries, as they high-five in your cranium. Then, like clockwork, your inner critic begins. You are not good enough for that job, you have zero experience, you don't even have a degree! Your job is fine. At least you have a job! Cue vision of you applying for the job and being rejected. There, take that! Now let's get on with your comfort zone. And just like that, you listen to the critic, you watch the pathetic show of your rejection, and you resign to doing exactly what you've been doing and not taking any steps forward on your journey. That is how we go through life, stuck in what we are doing and never taking leaps outside of our comfort zone. Heck, we don't even take tiny steps outside of our comfort zone because let's face it, we may fail and failure is scary on so many levels.

Now, what if your primitive brain laid dormant for a moment while you created your resume, submitted your application, and went for the interview? Wow, that would be a change, or what if you had the power to discipline the primitive brain and say, "Hey, hang on, before you call me names and show me clips of me failing, why don't you just wait a minute and let's see if I can prove you wrong?" When that happens, your new more sophisticated brain rejoices and gets all fired up with inspiration and now you have a battle of the brains. Primitive Brain vs. New Brain and it goes like this. Ding, ding, ding! In this corner is the Primitive Brain, the brain that holds you back based on fear of being eaten by a huge tooth-bearing animal, and all you have is a stick to defend yourself. In today's terms, you have a new opportunity that is arising, and the Primitive Brain has never seen it before, therefore, the Primitive Brain will pummel it and carry it back to the cave to eat it. Along the way, it'll explain why you don't deserve change and how terribly you'd fail if you even tried. This Primitive Brain is not going down easy and it's hold on your emotions is strong. It loves your comfort zone, for there is nothing to fear when you play small in the Primitive Brain. In the other corner, you have the New Brain, the brain that seeks opportunity and rejoices when you decide that you are moving closer to your true aligned self. In today's terms, you seek a new opportunity, and the New Brain cheers for you inside saying "you've got this, your resume is dazzling, and your dreams and desires are within reach." It's the side of the brain that inspires you and seeks alignment. The side that says "yes, break free from your comfort zone and soar ever higher". The battle begins and the argument ensues. Primitive Brain is calling you out and suggesting that you have zero skills, no reason for applying, and you're going to fail. Failure holds an emotional trophy and connects your thoughts to how you are going to feel when you fail and who you will be letting down and then the bell rings ding, ding, ding! Your emotional attachment to the fear of failing prevails again. Close resume, wake up at 6:00 am, drive to work at 8:00 am, and resume the unfulfilling life. That is exactly how it happens. Every damn time. Primitive Brain screws with your emotional attachment to your fears and discomfort and you can feel it take you to your knees and you settle for at least I have, fill in the blank.

Now, what if I told you that you have the power to swing back? Better yet, what if I showed you how to swing? This match would look very different if the Primitive Brain didn't have the power to tap into your emotions and bring fear in the ring. This is your chance to change it all around. Keep reading, we will get there!

> *Whenever you think or you believe or you know, you're a lot of other people: but the moment you feel, you're nobody-but-yourself.*
>
> — e.e. cummings

Chapter Two

The grip of perfectionism, guilt, and shame.

Perfectionism

*G*oing back to school in my 40's was so very different from my school experience as a teen. When I was younger, I was much more interested in my social life than grades, and honestly, I don't remember much of what I was taught during my teen years except for skills I learned from my friends. These usually included how to get out of the party before being caught. As an adult in my 40's with perfectionism as one of my traits, I strived for and "needed" to receive the highest grade possible all to tie back to the reward of a GPA of 3.98. I realize that this is ridiculous. That the grade does not define me, but man, perfectionism runs deep! Seriously, I would get very upset if my grade was below an "A." I was ashamed to share that with people, but because I never went to college when I was younger, I always felt less than those who did. I labeled myself as not being smart enough or good enough or valued. When I applied for jobs, I would try to highlight every aspect of myself so that others wouldn't notice that I had no degree. I would list my skills as bullet points and try to elaborate with lots of words so they would be too exhausted to get to the education section. When I had interviews, I would talk as much as possible about my experience, so they didn't ask about my education. I went in feeling like a loser and used my communication skills to charm people so they wouldn't ask about my college years. And frankly, based on what I had done in high school, I didn't get my education from books. I did all sorts of jobs to make enough money to support myself, but the striving to always need and want more and proving my self-worth created the perfect storm for perfectionism. I was always proving myself and rating my outcomes based on others. Self-judgement ruled my life and kept me in a vicious circle.

I now attribute my perfectionism or striving to never make mistakes to feeling like an underdog and fighting hard to get noticed. If everything I did was perfect, then my boss would notice me, my peers would notice me, my co-workers would notice me, I would notice me. Truthfully, I was struggling with the *I* part. Yes, I wanted to do well and glaze over my education piece, but honestly, if I was perfect, then I would value myself. Once I realized that this whole damn facade was to gain love and self-respect from myself, I realized that there was a whole shit-ton of work to do. I had to feel good about myself, *for me*. I had to decide how I was going to love all the parts of me – the stuff I'm afraid to share, the stuff I am struggling with, the stuff that makes me, well, me. If I wanted to like myself, I had to own every part of myself and love the good, the bad, and the ugly parts and realize that I am human. I have my own demons, we all do. I have made mistakes, it does not make me broken, or flawed, or unlovable. I am learning along the way, I am caring and worthy of my own love and the love of others and so are you. Now, I believe there are no mistakes, only lessons to learn in life. The more you learn, the more you fine-tune the version of yourself you want to show up as. The authentic self. The one you don't need to make excuses for, hide from, or devalue by playing small. The real you.

Perfectionism allowed me to hide behind dotting my I's and crossing my T's. If it looks perfect on the outside, then it must be perfect on the inside. Wrong! It is all a mask to cover up the real shit and walk around pretending you're all good when really, you feel a hole inside yourself. If this is you too, it's time to remove the mask or sometimes the many masks to find the real you and love who you are. With all the battle wounds and all of what you perceive as flaws, all the pain, and hurt. You are already beautiful and worthy of your own love and the love of others.

Paralyzed by being perfect and never moving forward.

When you are paralyzed by perfectionism, you may not see it for what it is. When I was at the highest perfectionism point in my life, I did not see it as a downfall. I actually saw it as a strength. I would highlight attributes on my resume like detail-oriented, dependable, can-do attitude, quick-learner, and achieve higher positions through determination. Those are all true and I am not dissing them. They are great attributes, but when you couple it with perfectionism, you actually create a situation where unless the work is perfect to you, it's not complete. When the work is not complete to your perfectionistic standards, you do not share it or want to show it to anyone, so you continue to improve and improve, and the task suffers. You have heard it doesn't need to be perfect, it just needs to be done. To a perfectionist like myself at that time, I'd agree, but not really for me. Yes, for others that's great and I will cheer you on, but for me during this time, if it wasn't up to my standards for myself, it wasn't done yet. Not only is it not done yet, but why can't I get it right? What is wrong with me? Why can't I get my thoughts exactly as I see them in my brain down on paper? Why does this font, color, slide, you name it, not look right? You see, it's not that at this time in my life I was judging the work of others, I was judging me. I judged my work so much that I was destroying myself inside but producing things that were of very high quality. And still, it's not enough. You know why? Because my core belief had nothing to do with the work I was doing. My core belief was that I was not good enough. Perfectionism and self-worth are old buddies. One says, "It must be perfect" while the other says, "**You** must be perfect." When you tie the two together, if you're not perfect in your eyes, nothing you produce will be either, and therefore, you are stuck, paralyzed in your imperfection. A way to grow from these unbelievable high standards is to shine the light on the area that is causing the pain. Shine the light on the area in your life that feels imperfect to you. My light was shining directly on my "I am not good enough" gremlin that I created. As soon as I decided to shine the light on it, I took the power away from the gremlin and faced the real issue. Why do I not feel good enough? It all tied back to self-worth.

Guilt.

As time went on with a full-time job, raising our son, our family life, and going back to school, my list of responsibilities grew and grew. I am a to-do lister to the max! If I didn't get a task done, I would judge myself and berate my wrongdoing. Guilt told me that I was not doing enough. I wasn't a good parent, good co-worker, good wife, good friend, good sibling, good daughter. Except for student. I was an exceptional student. It is true, If I wasn't receiving a grade from an outside source, I did not measure up. I did this to myself because I raised my own bar. I decided if I was getting an "A" for my responsibilities and in my mind I was not worth an "A". Heck, I wasn't even worth a "D". I could never reach my own standards because I allowed guilt to decide how good I was in any given domain in my life and guilt ruled, so I was floating around a "C" and that, to me at that time, was less than average and that was the filter I was viewing myself through. All of these realizations allowed me to step into my own power, but I had to discover the areas that were truly holding me back in order to step into my true self-worth and allow myself to see the greatness within.

Shame.

Now that we have defined the ways that hold us back, let's talk about shame. Ever hear yourself say "I should have?" Should signals shame. When I started journaling and reflecting to see if I could uncover some of my deepest desires, worries, and fears I ran into a lot of shoulds. I wanted to better understand myself and my personal rating system. As I was journaling, I started to uncover how much shame I carried. I *should* have gotten my degree sooner, I *should* have been a better parent to my son, I *should* have changed my career earlier in life, why am I in my 40's and am questioning my path? All of this and so much more reared its head in my journaling. It took time to untangle and realize that some of my shaming came from messages I heard from adults, the media, friends, and teachers until now and there is no judgment here. We often say things we don't mean or repeat things we have heard ourselves, but these messages told me that I *should* have had a handle on my life so that I could be more successful and not be questioning myself now. What is wrong with me? Replayed over and over in my head. Why don't I have a plan, and why does everyone else seem to have their shit together and I'm half faking it to fit in and assume my position in this world.

In our culture, shame is a scary word. We deny it, hide from it, and hope to hell nobody brings it up, but we all have it and we should understand how it arrived, and how to use a mirror to call it out. It helped me to better understand what shame is and how it arrived in my life in the first place. I love Brené Brown's books. In *Dare to Lead*, Brené writes "Shame is the fear of disconnection-it's the fear that something we've done or failed to do, an ideal that we have not lived up to, or a goal that we've not accomplished makes us unworthy of connection." Wow! When I read that, I was definitely on to uncovering a bunch of shame that was going on inside of me and how it was dictating how I was acting, feeling, and behaving.

Shame is an emotion that we feel when we believe or think we are seen as inferior to others. We are afraid of losing connection with others. Shame and guilt sometimes are confused and sometimes we just dump everything under guilt because we are taught at a very young age that shame is shameful. It's even hard to write about shame, that is how much I have been engrained to believe that it's a dirty word. Brené Brown also gives a great definition of guilt and shame to distinguish the two that I found very helpful. She states "Guilt = I did something bad, while shame = I am bad." We all have it, it's okay to uncover it, see it, reflect on it, and readjust your sails.

Where shame begins.

Shame most likely found its home in your psyche as a child. Messages were given to you when someone (usually an adult) is not pleased with your behavior. A parent saying things like, "Stop eating the cookies, you're already overweight", "Why can't you do better in school, what's wrong with you?", or "Every kid on this block rides a bike, you have two left feet and can't do anything right." The list goes on and on. Teachers may have criticized your work in school, an aunt or uncle may have commented on your clothing, size, hair, or the friend you hang around with. All of these messages that you received that you had no power over, create messages of shame. Why can't you be – fill in the blank. We internalize this information and believe the dialog of not worthy, not good enough, self-criticizing, and self-hatred. We feel that we cannot meet the needs of others, we are simply not good enough. That, my friend, is shame. We have all felt it, we know what it is, but we like to deny we have shame, and we like to stuff it down as deep as it can go, in hopes we never have to recall it, face it, or worse yet, confront it. Then we grow, and here we are, uncovering and dealing with loads of shame. We are so much better for learning about it and uncovering, and this is one key to freedom.

Catching ourselves when we speak with others. Are we shifting our perfectionism, guilt, and shame on them?

You have heard it, don't *should* on yourself or anyone else! When you use the word should you are creating shameful dialog. For example, I wake up early and decide to catch up on my calendar, but in my head, I hear, "You *should* be exercising". What am I really saying to myself? "Hey, what's your problem, why are you avoiding exercise? You ate a ton of brownies last night and you're gaining pounds by the minute." Shame, shame, shame. We are so used to shaming ourselves that we don't even see it or hear it anymore as shame. We see it and hear it as a voice reprimanding us for our behaviors. Those words are creating personal shaming. We all do it but catching it when it happens is the key. When we shame ourselves, we are using harsh words on ourselves and creating a destructive dialog about ourselves. Most people shame themselves without even realizing they are doing it because they are so used to having this dialog in their mind that they fail to see it as shame. Shame only creates more space between yourself today and your balanced, peaceful self you are working on becoming because it seems hard to attain what you really want in your life. After all, shame has you believing you are not worthy. The more shame, the more difficult it is to see yourself as whole. Once you face it head-on, you'll be able to pull it apart. For me, I had to journal about and stop being shameful of speaking about shame. We all have shame, it's okay to speak about it. The more we do, the less scary it is and the quicker we can pull it apart and move forward. Take out a journal or piece of paper and begin writing things you may feel shame around. Remember, shame is what your inner critic or gremlin is reminding you of how bad you are, how unworthy you are. Don't get confused with guilt which is about how you did something bad to another person.

We all have shame. It's okay to dump it out and add to it, so the light of day can shrink its deep-seated meaning in your brain. I will tell you that the first time I did this, I felt sick to my stomach. The word shame and the feeling physically hurt as I was uncovering these beauties, but here's the thing, we have to release them to release the pain inside. If we don't release it, it will live on inside of you eating you up and continually tell you that you are bad, not good enough, and not worth your dreams and desires. This is the real stuff that is holding you back.

Once I could see what was making me feel shameful, I could look at the list and pull each one apart, one by one. As soon as I started to do that, I not only felt more confident about myself, I saw each one as small, not so big anymore. Removing shame from our lives is like lifting a weight off of your shoulders and it puts things into perspective as to why certain things really trigger you.

"Do not wait: the time will never be 'just right'. Start where you stand and work with whatever tools you may have at your command and better tools will be found as you go along."

— Napoleon Hill

Chapter Three

Your schedule and to-do list are out of control and it's holding you back.

A to-do list is never-ending.

I have a to-do list and honestly, I am not sure what my days would look like without one. I cherish this thing because it's my roadmap to accomplish my tasks for the day and being a recovering perfectionist, this is the one area I have the hardest time allowing myself to loosen up. I love my to-do list. It sounds nuts, I know, but I create them sometimes just to have them. I use sticky notes and notebooks. I use scraps of paper (evenly torn, of course) and notepads. And, if I have a purple pen, it's perfect in my mind. I have spent years on accepting parts of my perfectionism that are beneficial and releasing the parts that are torture. I have read a lot of books on perfectionism and what it has done to my progress in life. I have made many strides, but man, the to-do list is my thing and so I have decided to embrace it. Here's the thing though. I embrace the act of writing down tasks, but I have learned to allow myself room to leave things unchecked. That is huge for me because I wouldn't be able to go to bed unless it was all checked off. Now, I say, "Okay, tomorrow the unchecked can move up on the list, or maybe I don't even need to do them. We will see tomorrow." And I put it away. That is a big deal for me and if you have a to-do list that runs your life, you know exactly what I am talking about. If you do not have a to-do list, sometimes it's helpful to stay on track with daily tasks and prioritize or reprioritize them as necessary. It's an easy way to keep track of life's stuff.

Let's talk about the never-ending to-do list that can be a trap. I shared with you that some things can be left undone and moved to the next day. I believe that, but some things you may have added just to add. I used to do this all the time because my perfectionism fed the desire to check stuff off the list to reaffirm that I was productive. You see, when you don't check things off the list and you are a perfectionist, it's hard to see accomplishment. So, I would add stuff just to check it off. I am not kidding you. An example would be to stop by my mom's to have coffee. Here's the interesting thing. Sometimes, I would add it after the fact and check it off. That my friend is a to-do list that is just reassuring your inner critic that you have done something, so you can check it off and call yourself complete for the day. The fear of not being complete would have me adding crap I already did! And that is why we add stuff to check off. Multiple checks equal multiple accomplishments which equal I am good, I am worthy, I am happy with myself. That damn checkmark acts as self-assurance, so the inner critic sees success. Red flag, a checkmark means nothing but a task done. It does not mean you are good, worthy, kind, whole, or anything else because you are all those things already. All it is, is a task done. When we use accomplishments as trophies for self-love, we miss the mark altogether. Our worth is not tied to any checkmark or trophy. Our worth is tied to self-love. If we rate ourselves on anything, we are diminishing our self-love. A checkmark is a checkmark, that's it. The symbolism of a checkmark meaning anything else is our story we make up to tell ourselves we are good or worthy. It's the story we need to work on, not the check marks or the tasks that you accomplish or did not accomplish for the day.

The never-ending task.

The never-ending task is the one you put on your list that has multiple steps to it, and when you see it, you ignore it and move to the next thing on the list because you know it is going to take time. Here's what to do with a never-ending task: Is it truly something you can do today, or do you need to break it down into smaller tasks? Here's an example of a never-ending task: Repaint the office. Now, repainting the office may take a week or longer depending on your schedule, your skill, and your desire to get it done. If you know the office repaint job is going to take a week, do not add it to your to-do lists every day as a huge task. Reason? It's too big, you will look at that huge task and skip it every time because we are wired to get things done. If it's too big to get done, you will do everything else instead of the big task because it simply cannot get done today. Instead of painting the office, write something like clean out the desk. Cleaning the desk is doable in an hour or so, you can get that done. Tomorrow, maybe it's clean off the top of the desk. Get it? Small tasks get done faster. You are more likely to clean out your desk than clean your office and paint it all in one day. You may even have to pick out a color, and we all know that can take days (even months)!

Prioritize your time into your list.

When you are prioritizing your tasks on your to-do list, what do you see? Are you placing the most important on the top or the bottom? Or are you like me and color-code your list? The reason I color-code my list with a highlighter is so I can see how many priority items remain later in the day, so I can check them off before evening, if possible. That is not always a great idea, however, because it flags anxiety right around 7:00 pm when I look at my list and still see pink highlighter. Here's a tip: allow unimportant (or low priority) items to transfer to a day where you have less to do or use a weekend list. I would suggest, if possible, no more than 5 items on your to-do list a day. Here's why - you still have other work to get done and too many items cause burnout. Keep the list short and to the point, break stuff down if you have to, move lower priority items to a day with fewer tasks, or for the weekend.

Exhausted, defeated, and still have more to do.

Your to-do list is sucking the life out of you, while you use it to feel accomplished. It's a lie. All it is is a list of yes, things to do, but things you want to accomplish (and much of it is made-up shit). To really get the stuff on your to-do list done, try to compartmentalize your tasks. Take easy steps and make them doable. Break them down. If you use a to-do list because you'll forget the things you need to do if you don't write them down, then that's a reminder list. We should distinguish the two. A to-do list is a thing you want to accomplish today, this week. Some people use a goal journal to go beyond this week such as this month, a year. Some planners are set up where you can write out your long-term goal to get them off your to-do list. Goals, especially long-term, are not to-do list worthy. They are goal sheet-worthy. Your to-do list ranks with priority. This is the shit you need to get done to move forward this week/today and feel accomplished.

Here's the thing, if you use your to-do list as your goal list and combine everything all together, you will never get shit done, and you will feel like a loser. The circle of guilt, shame, blaming will begin and you will be swallowed up in it. Separate the two. They are not the same. Create a new list. Put them anywhere, but not on your to-do list.

The opposite can be a problem too! If you're too busy doing things on your reminder checklist to even consider your dreams and desires because you've mucked it up with simple tasks, you lose sight of the big stuff. Just remember to keep your to-do list with actionable items that you can get done today or this week. Keep your goal list as items you are looking to achieve this month or up to a year. And if you must, a reminder list to keep them off your to-do list. Understand the difference and honor them all for what they are. Tasks on one list that are attainable (to-do list), desires for your life that you are working toward (goals), things that you need a reminder for (reminder list) like picking up your dry cleaning.

In a sea of stuff to do, steer your ship.

I like to pick two goals and keep them handy to help me steer my ship. I use sticky notes or sometimes I create reminders on my phone that remind me of my goals, but I always write them as if they are happening. For example, I have a reminder that pops up on my phone every day at 9:00 am. It says "Women around the world are inspired by your work," with a heart emoji. When I see this every day, it brings me to my visualization of meeting women who truly appreciate my gifts and are inspired by my message. I too am meeting women that I connect with on a deeper level, and they are inspiring me. These simple reminders are a powerful way to incorporate your goal into your day.

We stress a lot about where we are, where we are headed, and what we've done each day, week, month, year. I love the quote at the beginning of this chapter by Napoleon Hill, "Do not wait: the time will never be 'just right'. Start where you stand and work with whatever tools you may have at your command and better tools will be found as you go along." I love it because I have found it to be so true. Just start somewhere, anywhere and as you go the right people will show up, the ideas will come, the excitement will flow, and you will be on your way. Goals and lists work, but the true essence of arriving is not in the list, it's in momentum. The list just keeps you moving by checking things off. Stay moving, ditch what doesn't work, add what you find is working, but keep moving. The pieces will come together.

"Worrying is using your imagination to create something you don't want."

– Esther Hicks

Chapter Four

Don't sweat the small stuff.

Nobody cares!

*Y*ou have heard it before, I'm sure, but it's remarkable when you let it sink in – 85% of the crap we worry about, does not even happen. Some people say that percentage is even higher! So, those long restless nights, the nail-biting, and stomach-turning we put ourselves through, nope, does not even happen. You know why? We worry about what others think of us. Newsflash – nobody cares. Seriously, they are too busy worrying about themselves, you are not even a thought. But you'll stay up all night tossing and turning and overthinking things you said or didn't say. You'll beat yourself up with worry, fear, judgment, doubt, you name it, and they simply don't care. Why do we do this? Why are we so self-loathing that we create issues to feel sick over? Can we stop, please, stop? I know it's easier to hear than to do. I was a self-loather and sometimes I find myself in this hole too. To get out, I remember 85% of this stuff, nobody even cares about, so there is a good chance that this falls in there! And, if I am this sick about a situation, what does that say about me? These moments help me turn the light back on to myself to see if maybe I am the judger here. What is happening, really? Is this situation telling me that potentially, I am the judger, not the person or people I am truly worried about? Moments like this give us the opportunity to learn more about ourselves. Yes, every moment that arises that gives you pause, is most definitely a moment to learn more about yourself. Take time to listen, reflect and think about what is truly happening. There is no judgment, we must put that down and just listen and observe. Judgment is not going to bring you understanding. And it's not fair for you to judge everything you do because you are learning and evolving. We all are. We are not the same people we were when we were younger. We have more life experience, but we have held onto some of the old beliefs, so these moments allow us to examine them deeper to really figure out if they still serve us or not. When they don't, just ditch them.

How big is your mountain? Did it start as a molehill?

It was one of those 3 am mornings that I found myself rolling around in bed replaying the entire event in my head, word for word or at least the words that stuck. What was I thinking? What was he thinking? Why the hell did I freak out like that? Now I have to tuck my tail between my legs and apologize to my boss for my outburst. I feel so stupid. Oh my god, how could I have gone off on him in a meeting? Everyone must think I am a total loser. My colleagues probably went home and told their spouses that I called my boss a jerk in front of everyone. Holy shit! I called my boss a jerk in front of the entire team. Holy shit, I said he was a liar in front of everyone. I should probably just stay home today and look for a job. I'll call in and say I'm not feeling good, look for a job, and quit tomorrow. I can't face anyone. I am so embarrassed. That was me, about 15 years ago finally back in the workforce after staying home with my son for four years. It was the morning after an office meeting when my boss blamed the team for behavior that *he* modeled every day, not them. I decided to let him know that he was the person who was not being truthful, and he was the person that was responsible for all of the behavior in the office because he was the one actually doing it. Yup, you read that right. After he chastised us in a meeting, I shook my head and he asked if I had something to say. I said, "Yes" and then I proceeded to tell him he was being untruthful and a jerk because he was the one behaving badly. It still makes me uncomfortable to write about it. He dismissed everyone and stared at me for a moment, then stepped out of the room. I got hot and my palms started sweating and I felt like I was going to puke. My purse was at my desk, and I knew I needed to go get it and that meant walking past the staff and his desk. I went to the bathroom instead and waited, splashing water on my face, breathing, a little crying, telling myself that speaking up was good, then telling myself that speaking up was disrespectful, especially the way I handled it! Thinking about losing my job, thinking about my co-workers, and thinking about how the hell would I get out of the bathroom, get my purse and leave fifteen minutes early because I couldn't face anyone. I counted to five in my head and opened the door, walked down the hall like I was on a serious mission, grabbed my purse, and kept walking right out the door. Holy crap, I thought, as I opened my car door and drove my ass down the street to go pick up my son from preschool.

That night I told my husband everything that happened, and he agreed that the guy (my boss) needed to know, but I struggled with my delivery of such information. Then, I noticed a message on my phone. I listened to the message, and it was my boss. He asked to meet with me first thing the next morning. Here I am at 3 am, coming up with an illness that will keep me from having to go in and face him. I took a shower, drank way too much coffee, came to terms with the fact that I would be looking for a job, and dropped my son off at preschool. I drove to the office and walked into his office and sat down. I felt sick and a rush of resentment came over me and I felt like I needed to apologize for everything I said the day before and apologize to my co-workers and fix the damage I had done. However, in my mind, I was right. He was untruthful and a jerk and he deserved it and I was doing it to stick up for us, our team. As I sat there, I noticed that he looked nervous. I decided to allow that for a moment and then he opened his mouth. He told me that I was right, he hadn't been honest and kind of owned up to being a jerk. However, the next part of the conversation floored me. He was creating a new position and he wanted me to consider taking it. Wait, what the hell just happened? Alarms went off in my head, he was throwing out a salary to me that I could not turn down and I thought I was getting fired? I turned it down anyway and gave my two weeks' notice. Some jobs are not worth it in the end and I chalked this one up to one of those situations. Another lesson learned in life. It's hard to work with untruthful people whose egos tower over the largest of buildings. No thanks, I've got my own shit to work on, this was more than I wanted to be exposed to every day. Self-preservation, a good lesson and a great reminder that sometimes we worry too much over stuff that ends up completely different than we think. We have no idea how other people are interpreting a situation, so stressing about it does us no good. Sitting back and allowing a situation to unfold, not only allows us time and space to process the situation, but it also allows others to do the same. I still look back and wish I delivered the information differently, but hey, we all get a little hot at times and when it comes to values, sometimes, it gets really hot.

How we "see" things is not always real.

If we go back to understanding our beliefs, we will better understand how sometimes our beliefs get in the way of what we see in life. What I mean by that is if you are fully committed to a belief, you may be viewing a situation with that belief in mind and not allowing yourself to see it in another way. We see our beliefs as true to us, but that does not make them truth. There is a difference. True is what we believe to be true based on our beliefs and truth is the universal scientific truth of things such as your body is made of trillions of cells. You may believe that your body is made of jelly, but that does not make it truth. Just as you may believe that people who live in a certain part of the world speak with an accent, just as they believe you do. Our beliefs dictate how we see things and our perceptions translate what that is to us. Our belief may say, "The car you drive dictates your net worth." When we meet someone and their car is not a new model or they don't own a car, we may automatically jump to a judgement about them. However, we know nothing about this situation other than what we think we know. They may not place a high value on having a new model car, they may have made a conscious choice not to have a car, or they may have worked their butt off for the car they have. It's none of our business really, but we take the opportunity to pass it through our filter and judge a person based on what we believe. This is also how we treat ourselves. Ever wonder why those voices in your head pop up when you are about to do something really big, or after you did something that you were questioning? It's your critic or gremlin checking in with your beliefs then filtering it through your perception and dumping some seriously bad shit on your shoulders. If you believe that working hard is how you climb the ladder, and you decide to take it easy one evening, your gremlin passes that through its belief/perception filter and gets, "Hey, lazy ass! Yeah, you, get up and do something. How can you sit around and read or relax when we have shit to do?" Yup, that's how it works. But here's the good news. You can readjust the filter to have a better outcome.

Perception.

I think of perception as a kaleidoscope. Every experience we have encountered in life leaves us with a perceived outcome or feeling. We file these emotions and feelings with the memory of the experience in our minds. When a new experience happens, our minds automatically track back to see if it can match up the current experience with an emotion. This is how we decide at the moment how something makes us feel and ultimately what we do. If you are going to dinner in a busy mall and you once experienced a fire in a mall, you may have an uneasy feeling about being in a restaurant inside a mall. It is hardly the place you feel you can relax and when you arrive, you are looking for all the easiest escape routes. You may park close to the door, or far from the door if you felt trapped the last time. Now, picture being out at the restaurant with friends and a friend says, "I'll be right back, I want to grab a shirt from a store right around the corner." You begin to feel uneasy because you went over in your mind, over and over again, how you would direct your friends out the door and run to your car parked in an ideal spot to easily escape any harm. She grabs her purse and starts walking away. You jump up, "I'll go with you." You don't really want to go, but you don't want her to be left in the middle of a mall, unprotected if there were a fire. So here you are, we base all of our new experiences on previous experiences because we are wired that way, and sometimes, it saves lives. Sometimes, it's how we prevent getting into bad relationships, driving the wrong way home, taking a class that bores the heck out of you, and the list goes on. Sometimes it's great, sometimes it's not so great when you are about to do something new to leave your comfort zone and we freeze because of a past experience, or worse, we make it up in our head as an experience because we feel safer.

How do we separate the experiences so we are not holding ourselves back but still honoring our internal understanding of what may come this time based on what happened last time? Let's explore the kaleidoscope of perception a bit more.

In your own personal kaleidoscope, you have a piece of glass that represents an experience tied to an emotion. When you look through your kaleidoscope, you see many experiences coming together and many emotions mixed in with them. This view is your own personal kaleidoscope. You respond and react to everything in your life, dependent on your personal view, which is tied to previous life experiences. Nobody will have the exact same kaleidoscope, some may have similar experiences, such as growing up in a small town, or a parent's divorce at a young age, but we all attach our emotions to experiences in different ways. Therefore, each of us has our own personal perspective. That is why we can never truly say, "I know exactly how you feel." You don't. Nobody knows exactly how somebody feels at any moment. Each of us is so uniquely different, that we do not have any exact perspectives. Many people get confused or angry when others do not fully understand their perspective, but there is no real way to fully embody anyone's perspective because we are not them. We are us. We have our own personal experiences at certain times in our lives with different emotions attached to those experiences. We can have similar experiences and we can say "I understand how you feel", but we don't actually ever know exactly how somebody else is feeling. That is why we don't see eye to eye per se. We simply have different experiences. We can respect, listen, and understand each other's opinions, thoughts, and feelings and learn from them, but we are never in a place to say, "I know exactly how you feel." To better understand someone, try staying curious and asking more questions.

How to use the kaleidoscope to adopt new emotions for past experiences.

It is important to be able to understand why we feel the way we do in certain situations. For example, becoming an author was not on my radar. I felt that I was not ready to become an author because in my past experiences through messages I received, authors were very academic and loved to write. I do not feel super academic and in school, I disliked writing. I didn't love writing until I started journaling and I am 47 at the time of writing this book. When I decided to write how I felt and read a lot of other books, I realized that by being silent and keeping my thoughts to myself, I was not sharing my unique perspective with the world and something within these pages may spark a thought, an untapped well within others. If nothing more, maybe by being brave myself and putting my thoughts and ideas out there, I would live my life's desire of bringing others along with me, being brave for themselves too. Maybe someone else would be brave and together we could walk down the road of courage and share our inner thoughts and dreams. So, here I am changing the color of my glass in my kaleidoscope because now, when I look through it, I don't see self-doubt when I think of becoming an author, I see freedom to share ideas. You just decide to change the glass in your personal kaleidoscope and go with it. Nobody knows you did it, and it's quite liberating! It may take time and courage to do this but try to recognize when you are acting in a way that aligns with an old belief or experience. When you do, ask yourself if it still serves you? If not, change the glass and try seeing it differently.

We are not the center of everyone else's lives, they are!

Have you ever worried so much that you forgot why? Oh, my dear friend, I have. For some reason, we feel like we are the center of all life. By that I mean, everyone has eyes and ears on us. We feel like when we are walking down a road, every single person sees us, hears us, criticizes us, and actually cares that we are walking down the road. Wake up call, they don't! They care about themselves, not you. We are so self-absorbed that we honestly think that everyone has an opinion of us. Most people don't remember what you wore to work on any given day, but we will stand in our room deciding if we should wear the yellow blazer because we wore a color similar to the day before. Seriously, get over yourself. The sooner you realize that nobody cares what you wore yesterday, the sooner you can get out of your own damn way and get dressed, and head out the door. Why do we do this? We get in our heads and try to see what others think of us, so therefore, we project our own criticisms on others and harshly on ourselves. They don't care what you are wearing as much as they care what they are wearing! So, with that knowledge go out and try new things, shake up the apple cart, because nobody cares and unless you try something, you may never do it and if you know that they don't care, then do it – give it a shot. I promise you that when you try something different, it will feel strange at first, but not to them, to you. Then, you try it again and it gets easier and easier. Take small steps if you need to, or jump right in. But remember that when you stop doubting yourself, you will realize that nobody ever doubted you, except you!

"Dreams come with built-in challenges; challenges come with built-in dreams."

— Mike Dooley

Chapter Five

Digging deep –
What are your true desires?

*M*y true desire is to support others, like me, who struggle with self-doubt to convert their fear into power so they can transform their lives. I will do this by being authentic about my experience in my writing, speaking, and presence. A few years ago, I was afraid to tell anyone that because it seemed so far-fetched. My perception is based on my own self-doubt. I am a work in progress, just like you. We have to believe we have what it takes to pull this shit off or nobody will do it for us. We (you and I) are in this together. You have dreams and desires and so do I. Together we can give each other the courage to do the stuff in our lives that makes our soul sing. My dream is that once you get into this book, you'll head on over to **www.mandygrenier.com** and register to receive the downloadable worksheets that accompany this book, join my Facebook community, and stay in touch because this is how we grow; together.

How to uncover your true desires.

I always knew I wanted to support others. Like many of us, there is a fire inside of me that you can't snuff out. You know what you want to do, but if you're anything like me, you pushed it down because you were afraid of what others may think if you decided to change lanes. I remember having a conversation with a friend a few years ago and she asked me what I was doing now for work. I replied that I was enrolled back in college to earn a degree, and she said, "You never keep the same job, you change all the time. Why not find something and just do that?" When it comes to jobs, I actually do keep them for a long time, but my friend saw me doing other things outside of my job as never settling for something. For a few days, I was hurt. I felt that she was criticizing my work ethic and not knowing what I wanted in life. What was wrong with me was being replayed in my head over and over. Then, I started thinking about people in my life and she was right, everyone we knew stayed in their lane. Most had the same career since high school graduation or at least were in somewhat of the same profession. Not me, so what was wrong with me? It seems that we want to believe that you should know what you want to do forever, as soon as you turn 18. I jumped around like a rabbit from career choice to school to volunteer work, to travel, to professional development classes. I couldn't sit still and just settle for something. Once I allowed myself some space between the comment that hurt and the reality, I agreed with her, she was right. But why? Why was I never really comfortable in my job or life? After reflecting on this, I realized that at my core, I love supporting people in their personal growth. I, too, love to learn more about my own life. I have always reached out to provide support to someone in some way as far back as I can remember. Now, it's time to do that as a career, but before I was ready to commit to this new way of life as a career, I was still there offering my support to anyone who would accept it.

When you are thinking about your true desires in life, you probably already know what you want to do, but you are refraining from acting on it. Maybe because, like me, you had bills to pay and a kid to raise, family vacations, a life to live, and the norm to attain (the 9 to 5). What got me to where I am, is by doing it a little at a time. I knew I couldn't just leave my job and write or build online courses. I had to pay bills and a halt to our income for even a few months would have crushed us. But let's be real, it wouldn't be a month, I would need to build my business over time. So, instead, I got up early every morning and wrote, I listened to books and podcasts in my car, I read whenever I could, and signed up for any free learning I could get my hands on. I build my confidence through action.

Another side note: Surround yourself with positive learning modalities. As soon as you feel yourself sliding back, pop in your favorite author, mine is Dr. Wayne Dyer, or do something that brings you joy and helps you return to a positive outlook. Every time I hear Wayne Dyer's voice and listen to his books, I re-energize and feel whole again. Find your person or thing. I don't care if you dance, sing, run, listen to classical or rap. Find your thing and plug it in when you need a pick-me-up because it will happen. It's normal to go through ups and downs and want to push it all away because we don't want to make waves, or we feel it's too hard to change.

Another one of my favorite authors, I call him my mentor because I listen to his audiobooks and actually feel like I know him, is Gay Hendricks. If you have never heard of him, check him out. He has changed me for the better in so many ways. In Gay's book *The Big Leap,* he describes what he calls the Upper Limit Problem. Most people have heard of the comfort zone. Gay talks about feeling the uneasiness of the comfort zone and pushing beyond it. The upper limit is where you are pushing yourself past your comfort zone and breaking through the upper limit. I loved this so much because it explained the comfort zone as something to challenge and move past to push your upper limit a little higher, stretch it if you will. The more you break past the upper limit, the more of your potential you are tapping into. He also introduces his readers to the zone of genius. I fell in love with this notion because it helped me gain clarity about my own zone of genius and really owning it. I found that my zone of genius is understanding others' energy and emotion and meeting them with my own and raising it. I find that I have a gift to make others feel comfortable no matter the circumstances. Instead of just seeing that as a nice thing to know about myself, I am using that as my superpower. This simple realignment has changed how I interact, show up, and share myself with the world. What is your zone of zenius?

Don't play small – jump in, the world needs you.

When we play small, we are not only holding ourselves back but others as well. You see, when I discovered that my truest desire in life is to support others, I looked at what I was doing and thought, "I need to share more of myself to impact more people." By playing small all these years, I have actually negatively impacted others because I was not accessible. I have made it my mission to become more accessible to others, to share myself more, and to impact as many people as possible. In what ways can you increase your visibility? Think about how you show up. Think about your dreams and desires. Are you holding yourself back or ultimately are you not aligned with your true desires? I was definitely not aligned with my true desires. If my true desire was supporting others on a grand scale, but I was only accessible to a few, then I was holding myself back and not in full alignment. Think about where you may be out of alignment and see if there are ways you can improve upon your alignment with your true desires and your actual reality.

Our reality is made up of what we believe.

Here's the thing, we do what we believe we can do, period. If you believe you can run a marathon, you will train for it. If you believe you can sail the Pacific Ocean, you'll practice sailing. If you believe you can speak Mandarin, you will get a tutor or start a program to learn it. We do what we believe we can do. So, if you believe you can't run a marathon, then crash on your couch every night and binge-watch a show. If you believe you can't find your dream job, then don't look, or worse, look, but do nothing. You set your intention, which means, yes, my friend, you dictate how your life is going to go. Every step of the way. You have created your reality. Yes, if you are born into a difficult situation, it is not your fault and you may have to work a shit-ton harder to change your reality, I one hundred percent agree. What I am saying is no matter your reality now, you can make even small changes to impact your life for the better. Taking a walk, communicating with a friend, eating something you love, sharing time with a family member, taking a class to grow your knowledge on a subject, planting a garden, reading a book, growing a single flower. You can create something that changes your reality right now. At this moment, you can do something that brings you joy, and ultimately joy is where creating ideas springs from. If you're feeling stuck, find joy. If you're feeling down, find joy. If you're feeling pain, find joy. When we feel good, we exude good. It's a natural way of being. Try it, be happy and say something mean to yourself, it doesn't work. When you are happy and joyous you bring more happiness and joy to those around you and yourself. Our default setting is love, therefore, in happiness and joy we are returning to our true nature and through that true nature brings more love to share with the world. One tip I will share on this subject is that I am asked a lot, "How do you stay so positive?" The answer to that is raising my energy level. I think of times, places, and moments that bring me joy and it automatically raises my energy level to return positivity and joy into my life. I return to gratitude a lot and see almost everything as a gift. Try that. It works! When I am driving to work and I see a beautiful sunrise, I label it a "gift" and soak up its beauty. There are gifts everywhere, you just need to open your eyes, mind, and heart, to recognize that they are there and they are the spark to love and joy. See them and watch your energy shift. When you shift your energy you can shift the energy of those around you.

Your mind on autopilot and why visualization is so powerful.

You have no doubt heard of the conscious mind and the subconscious mind. This is a brief overview so that we all have a basic understanding of both.

Conscious Mind

We have all been exposed to, at one time or another, a basic understanding of our conscious mind. According to the Merriam-Webster dictionary, consciousness is "the state of being aware especially of something within oneself."[1] The conscious mind is the part of your mind that uses logic. It is our current awareness and includes things such as our perceptions, emotions, recent memories, and sensations. When you are asked a question, your conscious mind kicks in, goes through the checkpoints, and spits out an answer.

Subconscious Mind

The subconscious and unconscious mind are used interchangeably often when talking about our suppressed or repressed memories and experiences. This is the part of your mind in which you are not directly aware.[2] Most researchers believe that the subconscious mind is like a storage container waiting for the conscious mind to recall the information. It's like the vault of past experiences and memories. It's how you drive home without paying attention to the route. Subconsciously, your mind is wired to get you from point A to point B without having to be analytical about it. It's often explained as your passive mind. Many researchers also believe that this part of our mind is where our suppressed memories from trauma hang out. We don't want them sitting around in our conscious mind, so we suppress them and turn them away to our subconscious vault. Now here's the thing, it's from these memories and experiences that all of our habits, beliefs, and behaviors are formed. Now, why is this so important? Well, we can become more aware of these suppressed memories and emotions if we direct our attention to our subconscious mind. Within this area of your mind, you can unlock a lot of information and for many, begin a healing process to change their beliefs, habits, and behaviors. Repression, pushing emotions and experiences below the conscious level, begins early on in life, when you are limited on judgment and mental capacity.[3]

Let's look at it this way, if you experienced trauma and you attached an emotion to that trauma and called it fear, then as you are older and experience something that relates to that experience, you will recall the fear and ultimately, stay the hell away from it. But... what if you perceive something as fear when in actuality it is change? Let's give an example of this. You are 9 years old and your parents have decided to get a divorce. You are scared, upset, and feeling alone. The divorce is traumatic to you, and you understand those feelings are associated with the fear of losing someone in your life. You're 25 now, you are in a relationship and your partner is thinking of taking a job in Hawaii. You love the sounds of moving to Hawaii, but this experience is recalling a relationship loss, change of home, and brings up trauma for you. You decline to move with your partner, endure a devastating loss, and slip into depression. Repressed feelings surface when we experience situations that bring them to the conscious level. This is not fear of moving to Hawaii, this is trauma rearing its head when there is a decision to be made that involves a move, a relationship, and a commitment.

How our subconscious mind cannot discern if something is real or just an idea.

I'm sure you may have heard this and like me, it may have blown you away. Your subconscious mind cannot determine what is real and what is made up. And, if you have been following along with how you call up experiences from your subconscious mind to direct you in how you are going to respond to an issue, behave, think, or act, well, now you can see how we may misconstrue things, but now you understand why visualization works so well.

Many athletes use visualization and credit it when they achieve a high level of success. Researchers have shown that thoughts are just as impactful, if not more, as actual training.[4]

Holy cow, right? It is truly amazing when you think about it. You can visualize and manifest what you desire. How can this help in your life? Visualize what you want to see, do, experience in your life. Do it to train your brain to live in the feelings, emotions, and sensations of all that you see for yourself in your life and watch how your life changes. These images, emotions, and new beliefs are stored in your subconscious mind. I am not suggesting that all you have to do is visualize yourself winning the lottery and it will happen. No, I am not, but I am suggesting that when you visualize yourself living the life of your dreams, you are moving the fence for your gremlins who respond to the thoughts and beliefs that live in your subconscious mind. They don't know if you have achieved it or not. They just want to hold you back from something you've never done. As soon as I began visualizing this book, I wrote more. I saw myself finding an editor, a designer, and being asked to speak about fear and how we can dismantle its grip on us. I visualized meeting new people, traveling the world. As I write this now, I have spoken with editors and have begun the process of bringing this book to life and into your hands. No longer am I saying "someday", I am now saying "today, yesterday, tomorrow." You can bring life to your dreams and desires, believe they are here, act as if you have already received it, visualize yourself in the moments of achieving your desired outcomes and watch it all unfold!

> *Once I had asked God for one or two extra inches in height, but instead he made me as tall as the sky, so high that I could not measure myself.*

— Malala Yousafzai

Chapter Six

Learning to love and trust yourself.

*W*hen you look at the sky, do you feel as though you can touch it, maybe not yet, but you will. At first, it is scary to fledge the nest and love and trust yourself. This is because we have been given messages throughout our life that we must be validated by others first to gain confidence in ourselves. Your earliest memories may be of seeking acceptance from your parents, siblings, friends, and extended family members. I remember trying to win the approval of my two older siblings a lot. I was the youngest and wanted to be in the middle of everything. When our cousins came over, I and the other youngest cousin were called "the babies." We were not permitted to play with the older cousins, so we would follow them around and hide in places they didn't know we were in, so we could listen to them as they chatted about music, television, and whatever else they felt was "cool" at the time. Seeking approval is something we all do. When we are denied approval, it reinforces our feeling of not being good enough, not being worthy, or funny, or accepted. It starts with small, silly things like chasing your older siblings and your cousins around and it goes on through a lifetime of approval-seeking to fit in. Middle school is an example of one of the harshest environments for peer approval. Everyone wants to be in the "in crowd", but nobody really knows what that represents. We just want people to like us. We want to feel as though we belong. Over time, our approval-seeking behaviors tell us that unless others like you, you don't amount to much. We lose our sense of trust in ourselves because we really only want others to "see" us as being worthy. We no longer rely on our own senses, because we are too caught up in how our actions will be perceived by others.

Trust in ourselves seems so far away, yet we listen to our gut instincts on many issues. We know it's there, but it's the confidence to trust ourselves that gets mucked up. Can you think of a time that you trusted your friend's instincts over yours? I can! There have been many times I overrode my own trust in myself to place it in the hands of others. It happens, we want acceptance. We take jobs we don't like, we date people we are not really into, we hang out with people we have lost interest in, we say "yes" to stuff all the time that we really don't want to do. Why do we do this? Many people say it's guilt, I think it's acceptance. If we say "no," we may lose that person in our lives and we want them and others to accept us. Remember when we talked about shame in Chapter Two? Loss of connection equals shame. We give parts of ourselves away every day. We hold on to very little and wonder why we don't trust our inner voice or love the person we have become. We have trouble saying the words "I love you" to ourselves because it feels inauthentic. I remember listening to an audiobook by Dr. Edith Eger. She's an amazing woman, if you have never heard of her, acquaint yourself! There is a part in one of her audiobooks where she talks about saying "I love you" to yourself. I had done this exercise before at workshops, but doing it that time, I sobbed. You know why? Because I wasn't sure I really loved myself just as I was. I actually knew I didn't and that is why I sobbed. The shame of using alcohol to cope with stress and perfectionism and not living up to the stuff I thought I *should* be, held me so tightly that I didn't even like myself at times. I wouldn't call me up to say, hey, want to hang out tonight? Because I was losing control over who I was becoming. I felt lost, scared, and really, really sad, but nobody knew. They knew I liked having fun and having a few glasses of wine, and that I was somewhat of the life of the party. Nobody knew that I did that to escape from the stuff I was afraid of. Learning to trust my inner voice, the one that said, "Now is the time to stop and embrace the shit to move forward with love," was hard. Learning to love the person I am and was becoming, was hard, but it got easier the more I was real with myself and others. I had to reframe my thoughts and sit with the pain to finally allow myself to forgive myself and love who I am. This stuff can take years, this stuff can take days, we create our own path to healing, I knew I had to turn shit around quickly in my life because I was not living the life of my dreams and I wasn't sure at that time if I would ever achieve that. The feeling of knowing you have the opportunity to be all that you are worthy of being, but not trusting that you have what it takes to become what you see for yourself, takes courage. The kind of courage that comes with self-love.

What does it mean to love yourself?

Loving yourself is the greatest gift in life because once you truly love yourself, you can fully express love to others. For me, I became much more open with my feelings and allowed myself to explore thoughts and ideas that I never would have allowed before. Forgiveness for others and yourself is a huge step to loving yourself. When you fully feel that you love yourself, you express love in so many new ways. You may stop and listen to birds a little longer, take some time to watch the sunset, give yourself time to take the walk, run, bike ride, or maybe it's allowing quiet time, picking up the phone to chat with a friend. I decided to pour a lot of it into self-reflection, slowing down, going within, and, ultimately, pouring myself on the pages of this book. This is because I know that writing is part of my healing and by loving myself, I am allowing myself to fully understand myself, and I am allowing others to truly see me for who I am. The only thing that matters is that I love myself. I know that now. I understand that saying, "I love you," to yourself in the society and culture that I grew up in, sounds egotistical. It's not. It's actually a fuller expression of yourself towards others. You show others how you feel inside. When you feel pain, hurt, sadness, shame, guilt, doubt, you show up with those emotions, that is why I used wine to cover it up. All it did was splash paint on a dull, sad, and confused surface. Others see what you give. When you show up with self-love, you show up with love for others too.

Meditation can bring peace and assurance.

Meditation is allowing yourself the space to focus your attention inward. That's it. Many people get weirded out when you mention, "I love meditating." Here in Western society, it took time for us to catch on. I remember when yoga and meditation became "a thing." It wasn't that long ago that we used to wear brightly colored spandex, headbands, and leg warmers, and jump around adding a few leg lifts in the mix, then yoga and meditation entered the room and people were questioning the hippies that brought it to the gym. Now it's everywhere, in classrooms, living rooms, on television, on beaches, even in airports! People are practicing yoga everywhere. When I first started my meditation practice, I felt like it was so hard. My mind wandered, I began thinking of laundry, dinner, my to-do list, my work, you name it, the silence brought more mind chatter. Over time I have learned to allow the thoughts to arise and allow them to go. Sometimes I will say, "I hear you, as soon as I am done, I will get to you." That allows me to acknowledge the thought but dismiss it at the same time. I did not know, however, that this was normal. I thought it was me and I was broken and could not meditate. I think this was because everyone I saw in a photo, online, or on television meditating looked so peaceful and still. I was pushing my cat off me, thinking of all sorts of stupid things, and could never maintain the beautiful balance they were able to hold. My legs would get numb, and I'd start saying okay, I should probably end this because I'm bored. Bored! Yes, I remember thinking, I am bored. Anyway, over time, meditation (stick with it) will become your safe space. The place you can retreat to for self-love, acceptance, and balance. To begin, just sit in silence and focus on your breathing. That's it. Start slow. I love meditating in my backyard just past the tree line. In those woods, I feel relaxed. The chances of being interrupted are few. Some people find it easier to focus with spa music or classical music, try it if you'd like. There really is no right or wrong way to find inner peace and tranquility. The purpose of meditation is to reduce stress, slow down the mind, and focus inward. Meditation has wonderful health benefits too. I use it to find inner peace and balance and to allow myself space to just be. Try it, see what you think and if you want to add it to your routine, give it time and give yourself time also.

Remember, the goal is to love yourself first so that you can spread your love and joy to others. Truly, in this life, you really only have you – everything else is temporary. I know that is a scary thought, but it's true. You have zero control over anything, including anyone, except you. You are here to stay with you, so find love for yourself, do it whole-heartedly and watch how much you express love more freely to others. Ever hear someone say, "I live for you" or "you complete me"? Sometimes we say things and then later you look back and cringe, but here's the deal – you live for you and only you can complete you. You are whole just as you are. Family, friends, co-workers, significant others are gifts in our lives. They desire that you love yourself because when you do, you can fully express love with them. To be present and be in harmony with your life, you must love the person you are or heal the areas that are causing you pain. When we do, we fully express our authentic selves and can extend it to others.

Vulnerability.

We are so afraid to let others see us. It's another area that we attach fear to. If people really know me, they may not like me, they may judge me, they may talk about me, they may see flaws. Well, guess what honey, we all have flaws. In fact, that's the good shit. The not-so-perfect, not practiced, no make-up, messy stuff makes us real. When we are afraid to share our uniqueness, we keep it to ourselves and stay fenced off from others. What the hell is perfect anyway? We don't even know because nobody knows. It's made up. Fake. Let's not be fake, okay? Vulnerability is showing up as you, authentically. We are so wrapped up in approval that nobody really knows us. It took being extremely vulnerable to put myself out there in the pages of this book. I'm proud that I did because vulnerability is courage. Not everyone will appreciate it, that's okay. I don't need approval from everyone, I'm past that now. How about you? How much do you really share of yourself, your real self? When you open up to others, you show the world who you really are and you permit others to open up too. I see being vulnerable as being real. I like real.

Understand and identify your core values.

Using your values to readjust your sails in life is the first step in trusting ourselves. Identifying our core values is key. To do this, just grab a piece of paper or use your journal to list up to ten core values.

Here is mine:

- *Family*
- *Connection*
- *Personal Development*
- *Kindness*
- *Expansive Energy*

- *Courage*
- *Spirituality*
- *Adventure*
- *Authenticity*
- *Dependability*

Your list will be different depending on your core values. Once you know (or begin to know) your values, you can adjust your sails. You can even whittle the list down to a core few, say four or five. In my example, I know that family is a core value of mine, therefore, when a decision or situation arises, I can come back to how the situation fits with my core values? Does it honor my value of family? Example: I am invited to a party, however, my family is having a BBQ the same day. I feel torn because another core value is dependability and sometimes, I confuse the two of being dependable and being a good friend. If you ask me to do something, sometimes I feel as though I have to do it because I am dependable. So, how do I untangle this? First, I look at the possibilities of my schedule. Can I reasonably do both and feel fulfilled or am I racing around and eventually just causing stress therefore I cannot be present in either situation and I am no longer being authentic? Yikes! Another core value will be invoked in this situation. Okay, I have determined that I cannot reasonably do both based on timing and therefore, I must choose one over the other. I want both, but I can only do one and I must feel confident in my choice, or I will be upset all day and feeling resentful. I ultimately chose the family BBQ. I chose the family BBQ because even though I love my friend and I don't want to miss her party; my core value of family would eat at me all day. Ultimately, I would not be happy. Now, there are plenty of times that I went the other way, but I went through these steps. There have been times that I went to a family BBQ the weekend before, so I chose the friend's party because I wanted to do both but needed to find a way to achieve that without going out of alignment. So, I came up with an alternative to do one thing this weekend, and another next weekend. I have also missed out on family things because of work, school, other engagements because I placed dependability on top for that particular situation. This is why judging is not helpful to anyone because you do not know their core values and you have no idea how they got to the decision they made for themselves to stay in alignment with their true self. The most important thing is to understand what your core values are so that you can make decisions in your life that align with your true self. Take some time to get familiar with writing about yourself if you have never done an exercise like this before. When you are comfortable, come up with your core values. Sometimes mine change, depending on where I am in life. Some values may appear or disappear. Instead of beating myself up now, I accept that I am ever-changing and it's okay to adjust as you grow. For example, excellence was a core value of mine. I believed I always had to achieve excellence in order to be self-fulfilled. After doing much work around core values, I realized that for me, excellence was placing a very high expectation on myself that felt self-defeating, not self-fulfilling, so excellence was dropped. For some, excellence is a core value and if it is, go ahead and honor it. For me, I confused my perfectionism for excellence and ultimately it was the source of my non-doing and highly judging, self-stress-induced life. I was feeding perfectionism with excellence and accepting it as a piece of my identity. I had to adjust or I'd still be spinning on why this book isn't done yet.

Use your intuition.

Intuition is a funny thing for some people. Others wholeheartedly believe that they can tap into their intuition, and it can lead them to greatness. For clarity, I am on the latter. Intuition to me is your inner voice. It can lead you to greatness, but if your entire life you have stifled it, it may take time to rekindle your relationship. Either way, it's okay as you are in the perfect spot in your life to start listening and getting curious about what it is saying.

Let's begin with what intuition is. Intuition is a knowing without going through an analytic process to understand something. We've all had the experience of having something just not feel right or doing something because it did feel right. Maybe you bought a home because you had a "good feeling," or you left a party because something didn't "feel right." Maybe you heard a voice, we sometimes call it our "inner voice" that suggests you take the job, or leave the job.

That voice is your higher self talking to you. However, we must be clear on how intuition and bias can be intertwined.

We all have biases, good or bad. Yes, a bias can be good such as choosing to believe a healthy lifestyle will benefit your life, therefore you eat healthy foods and exercise regularly. However, when we begin to judge others based on our biases these seemingly good biases can also be very harmful. How does a bias get routed in our way of being? Bias is programmed into our being by the messages we receive from our family, society, and culture. The outcome is that instead of learning more about a person, we use a mental shortcut to infer our own judgment. The shortcut goes through our bias filter, and we make a split-second judgment based on our own bias. We then create the story in our head about what we are seeing. Therefore, we must understand if the inner feeling is based on bias and judgment or inner guidance.

How do we do this? We get analytical about the "feeling." When our intuition tells us something, ask yourself if the "feeling" you have is because of your own bias filter or is it an inner knowing. Once you check the "feeling", you can usually get an answer. If not, get curious. Why did I feel this way? What came up for me when I had this feeling? Did I see someone, something, or react to a bias rather than allowing guidance to flow through me from my higher self? It is a wonderful way to achieve even greater clarity around our biases. The best part is that we get to choose if we want to keep those biases or dismantle them. I love that work. It is my favorite part of growing as a human. The hard work is the most rewarding. We are not putting ourselves under a microscope to examine, judge, shame, and hurt ourselves. We are doing this work to unveil areas that are holding us back or causing our thoughts, feelings, and physical being to be out of alignment with ourselves. This is the work of authentic self-love. Digging deep to open the vault of pure love. The stuff trapping us is the judgment, shame, guilt, unhappiness, and lack of self-love and trust. We get to peel that back and emerge our authentic selves. It is up to us to do the work to create the being we know we are and truly want to be.

Guidance from Spirit.

When I speak of Spirit, I refer to it as any guide from another realm. For some it comes in the form of relatives who have passed, an inner knowing, energy derived from creation, some also call it God, Spirit, or the Universe.

Have you ever asked for guidance from spirit? I do it all the time, it's okay! Pray, meditate, ask to call spirit in, or simply talk with spirit. When you do, you open up channels for spirit to reach you. Some may find this too far down the woo-woo track to classify as a skill, but I don't. I love communicating with my angels and by doing it, I feel more confident and connected to my past, present, and future. My spirituality.

Here is a simple exercise on how I talk to what I call "my angels" which are relatives who have passed. I often ask them for guidance. Normally in the evening, when I am getting ready for bed, I get very quiet. I lay still and because I am a crystal lover, I am usually holding a crystal. I take 5–6 slow deep breaths and listen to my breath as it goes in and out. After those slow deep breaths, I return to normal breathing and continue listening to the air from my breath go in and out of my body. I then picture a few of my family angels, those who have passed, and see them each and say their name. I have some family members that I have never met that I feel deeply connected to, so I normally see them as they look in a photograph that I have of them. My grandfather that I've never met, I see him a lot as pure energy. However, they appear, it is okay. You may only see light or a swirl of light or energy and not a face. I believe this is because we are all energy, and we return to our energetic state. My grandfather is strong in his energetic presence for me and that is how he presents. Now that I have seen them, and said their names, I usually ask for guidance on an issue. Not looking for an answer, just stating the situation and then asking for guidance. Sometimes the guidance comes right away, sometimes it comes over time, but I know they have my back – so to speak! Other times, I just want to connect and feel their powerful presence and let them know that I am fully connected to their spirit. I understand that some of you reading this book may find this a bit too far out there, but I encourage you to allow yourself the time and space to connect to spirit and see how it makes you feel. If nothing else, you are opening up the channels of energy and allowing yourself time to breathe, reflect, and renew.

Here is an example of how this angel connection has worked for me. My entire life, I have been told that my mother's dad was an alcoholic and that he died when my mom was only nine years old. When I was younger, the stories I heard about him actually scared me and I had no feeling of connection to him at all, nor was I seeking the connection. As I got older, however, I began thinking about my grandfather and was curious about him. I began allowing him to come to me and opened my channel of communication up with him. All I felt was gratitude from him, no facial picture, nothing, just an overwhelming feeling of gratitude and acceptance. It was strange to me that I didn't feel scared, or uneasy with his energy. I had heard a lot about him and was a little apprehensive of connecting with him.

Not feeling uneasy with his presence, it made me wonder if I was intentionally cutting him off from my intuitive energy channeling with him because I was angry about what my mom, her siblings, and my grandmother felt. I then began to forgive him. I told him I wanted him with me, I wanted his presence to show up, to guide me. He was there. How do I know? His energy gave me the strength to release alcohol in my life. I feel positive about this. When I was struggling with my addiction to alcohol and wanted a change, I did the exercise above, laid in silence, and called him in, he came. I asked him for his strength to change my desire for alcohol. His energy was surrounding me while I was going through my hardest days. He's still here in fact. I know it because I get an overwhelming feeling of love when I think of him. Remember, I never met him, but I feel his presence all the time. All I did was allow him to connect with me, and he's an ever-present energy field of love that surrounds me. Open your channel and receive the love and support from spirit. The connection is beautiful and when you feel it, you'll know.

66 *Taking risks doesn't mean throwing ourselves blindly into danger. But it means embracing our fears so that we aren't imprisoned by them.* 99

— Dr. Edith Eger

Chapter Seven

Using fear to propel you toward your dreams – Freedom Superpower!

This thing we call fear, I call its bluff.

Your entire life you heard the word fear as a negative word. We attribute anything that gives us discomfort to fear. If you are thinking about changing careers you may tell someone, "I am fearful that I am too old" or "I am afraid I am not good enough in that field." The list of gremlin voices goes on and on. The issue is this: are we really afraid, filled with fear, or are we uncomfortable with the idea of changing something up in our lives? Let's flip that around and see how fear is a nudge, if you will, in the direction outside of your comfort zone or, as Gay Hendricks writes in his book *The Big Leap*, your Upper Limit Problem.

I love this concept because this is how I went from the feeling that I was settling in life, to getting my degree, releasing alcohol, writing a book, becoming a coach, the list goes on. When we change the way that we see this thing we call fear, we understand fear is the key to propelling your life forward in any direction you wish to go. This perspective unlocks your responses and helps you realize that sometimes these fear messages are messages of greatness. Let's be clear, when I first started thinking about fear and stepping toward it, it was not super comfortable. I didn't like it at all. Everything I have ever learned in my entire life was that when you get close to fear, run like hell. But that again was just other people in my life projecting their fear onto me and others. When we are in a place that feels uncomfortable, rather than running, allow yourself to listen to the "fear" and understand what you are truly feeling. I am not speaking of physical pain or someone running after you, or a dog showing its teeth. I am talking about the fear messages you hear inside when you are thinking or about to do something outside of your comfort zone. Anything that brings you reluctance when stepping into the unknown. Dig deeper when this comes up for you and ask yourself, "Why am I reluctant to go in this direction?" The answer you receive will be your key to taking fear by its hand and walking with it, instead of away from it.

I believe that when you feel fear it is actually your higher self speaking to you through intuition. Try not running away from it, try not even calling it fear. Try moving towards it, try to listen. When you go from, "I am afraid, scared, fearful," to "This is a sign that I am going to a place that I am unfamiliar with," then you no longer feel fear. Instead, you feel opportunity and excitement and now you can begin to understand your apprehensions. This is where the real change in life comes from.

Rather than running from your fear, and avoiding it, you can walk beside it and listen to it. But you need to know when it's pushing you toward greatness or pushing you away from your true self.

Greatness feels scary sometimes, especially when we have not seen it in ourselves, or we doubt we have the ability of greatness. For me, this feeling comes up in my gut. Feelings can come up in any part of your body. For me, doubting myself, I feel square in my gut. It feels like a pit in my stomach, it's actually very uncomfortable. You know the feeling, you either need a bathroom quick or you could puke or pass out. When I get that feeling, along with the gremlin saying, "No, this is too high level for you, let this pass, you are not good enough," I step back. Or at least I used to step back. By step back, I mean, actually run from the discomfort and return to my normal (comfort zone). Now, I listen to this feeling and the gremlin. I sit with it for a moment and acknowledge it. I even talk to it, not kidding! Here's what I say: "Hello, fear or self-doubt, I feel you and hear you. I am going to do this anyway, so you and I will walk together on this. Thank you for showing up, because when you do, I know I am headed in the right direction. Your intention is to protect me. I am ready to go into the unknown." That's it. I acknowledge, am grateful, and ask it to join me on the journey. Sounds too simple right? It's all good. And you're right, it is very simple! Here's the thing, once you acknowledge it, you stop fighting it. That is the key. Internally, you are fighting the feelings of, "I want to try, I think I can do it, but you will suck at it, you're not good enough" crap that is all lies, just to keep you small and in your comfort zone. That fight inside of you is causing the issue, not fear, we just call it fear. When you acknowledge and listen to it, you give it a name and you accept that you hear it and you're willing to accept the temporary discomfort for the payoff. And, when I do this, miraculously, that pit feeling subsides. My body now has been signaled by me that we are okay, I am in control, it can stop showing me signs of danger. There is no real threat, just my gremlin talking me down. I've got this.

How to tell the difference between greatness and being pushed outside of your values.

Greatness feels scary at times but living outside of our values feels even scarier. Let's say you are in a situation where you are asked at work to do a task that you don't feel aligns with your core values, such as lying to a customer. You know the feeling I am talking about. Your supervisor insists that the product will bring XYZ and asks you to pass that information along to your customer, but your experience has shown otherwise. This is living outside of your values. Some of us chalk this up to work-life, not my real life. I can do this at work because I am being paid and I need the job. Others say, "No way!" and refuse to live outside of their values. That feeling that you get there has its own way of showing up. For me, this has shown up in my head. Literally, I have had to stop, relisten to the request, pass it through my value filter, then be quiet and allow my body to feel what it is being asked to do. When I feel the heat flare up in my head, I know what to do. The signals from your body are flags and directions. They are not something to fear. They are allowing you to make decisions based on passing the information through all of your checkpoints. We all, however, have different checkpoints based on our beliefs and previous experiences. If you had been exposed to using untruths early in life and it didn't seem like a big deal, you may go right along with the request even if it felt a little wrong. Your alarm bells did not ring. Your supervisor may have been taught this way too and after doing it a few times, their sales were sky-high. For them, the value was security, not truthfulness. We all have our values and beliefs. This is how one person can see something so different from another, but still care deeply about the other person. Some of our values and beliefs overlap, others are way off. Understanding how this works also allows us to have empathy for others. Your ideas and their ideas may not match up in fact, they probably won't based on all of their life experience and yours, but there is usually a middle ground where we can all relate and work together.

Now that we understand that the feelings we receive in our bodies when we are experiencing discomfort actually tune us into greatness or living outside of our values, we get to choose how to use that superpower. Rather than calling this superpower "fear", let's call it "freedom". We all have it, we all can access it, we all can put it to good use. Your freedom superpower will show up in feeling (gut uneasy, head gets hot, hands sweat, feeling flush), thoughts will ensue (sometimes in the form of gremlins) and, at that point, you have a choice. You can acknowledge your freedom superpower and respond. You can thank it, name it, and ask it to walk alongside you. You can turn this thing we call fear into your best friend, literally. I know, I have done it and I am not the only person who has written books on this, shared how-to videos, offers courses, etc. We all have this power, we all can access this power, we all can use it for our greatest good.

~~Fear~~ Freedom is your best friend.

You see, this thing we used to call fear is the only way we communicate with our bodies when something arises out of the normal day-to-day in our lives. Your body responds, we react. You have the ability to retrain your brain on how to respond. We do not want our bodies to stop telling us when something is outside of our norm. We need that. It's all in what you do with it that counts. It's about learning the language of fear.

When I was about to give birth to our son, I started thinking about my job. I thought I would just go back to work full-time and find a sitter for him. After he was born, it was so difficult to leave him. I cried every time. I interviewed I don't know how many sitters to try to find the right one, but inevitably, none were going to work for me. I was sabotaging these visits. Because I knew I did not want to return to work and leave my son. It could have been Mother Teresa and I would have found something about her that flagged me. It was almost ridiculous, and my husband knew when I would tell him about the places I had "checked out" that there was no way in hell that I was going to leave our son anyway. My job provided our healthcare, so I knew I had to go back, and I loved my job, so we had to figure this one out. Every night I would struggle with this choice. I had healthcare being provided by my employer, I was bringing in an income to help our newly formed family. Leaving this amazing job would also mean that I probably would not return, and I loved it. But leaving my son was so strong an emotion that every time I thought of it, I was torn up inside. After weeks of agonizing over this decision, I decided to leave my job. My gut hurt by this time because every time I thought about leaving, I would hear the voice inside saying, "You can't leave, you don't have the income, the health benefits, your family will go into so much debt" and "if your family struggles it's because of you." My stomach was in knots every day while I was also overjoyed to be spending time with my son. Values were being tested here. It was a time of complete opposite emotions working against themselves causing my body to physically hurt. During this time, I was labeling this as "fear." I would say things like, "I am so afraid to fail", "I am so scared that we will lose everything because of my desire to be with my son", "if we end up bankrupt, it's my fault", "I should have stayed in my job", and "I am afraid of screwing this up for my family." This went on and on for at least six months. On the other hand, my son and I were bonding, and I knew inside I made the right choice. I also felt I was putting us in financial ruin. I was scared. If I stayed at my job, we would have healthcare and an income. Now I am counting dollars at the grocery line to make sure we can afford what is on the conveyor belt. It was a scary time in our lives and the voices in my head were loud. I am no stranger to fear, I have struggled, held bills to pay later, and taken up part-time jobs in the evening to make ends meet. I know this fear, however, I also had the courage to change the way I saw this situation. I decided to walk with this thing in my head I called "fear." I invited it in and asked it to show me a better way without losing my time with my son. I decided I wasn't going to feel sick anymore or place blame on myself because of my choice to be with my son. Financially, we found our way back. But by acknowledging the fact that I felt sick because of this fear I carried around with me like a battle scar and fed the voice of, "I am not good enough, I put our family in this situation, and I must figure it all out on my own and be punished for my doing", I was able to see my way out. I was able to label the fears I had and find a way to work on them individually. Most of this fear came in the form of shame. I am not good enough, came up daily. When I worked on that, I was able to separate what I was calling "fear" from the real reason I had these emotions. I do not need to be punished for my desire to be with my son. My husband and I made the choice for me to stay home. Once I began to pull it apart, I found solutions. I took a part-time job to offset some of the bills, and we found ways to close the gaps. Over time, we adjusted our lifestyle and made it through those days. And now, looking back, I wouldn't have changed a damn thing. It was scary at times, it even made me feel physically sick, and I did some serious damage to my self-worth, but because of all that, I learned that there is always a way, if you stay open to it. Our family values matter, and we got very creative with making great things with little means. Until I looked at fear in the face and accepted that this was not going to take us down, I used this to get stronger. You can too. It is within us all. We all have this power and you have probably done it before without even knowing what you were doing. Your superpower is alive and well inside of you, when you give it the power, super things will happen. You'll see!

Now, sometimes like in my story, the fear you feel can be because of other circumstances such as the fear of losing your home or putting your family in financial ruin. However, when you pull that apart, it's still not really fear, it's disappointment. I was worried about disappointing my family. I was worried that my choice of leaving my job was causing the pain of my family losing everything we had. I built up a lot of guilt and shame around that decision and beat myself up for my choices. Nobody else did that. When I began digging deeper and naming it for what it was, I was able to work on those specific areas in my life to gain control back and work little by little to make changes that ultimately set us back on course. In my opinion, it also moved me so much further along in my own self-awareness.

This thing we call "fear" lets you know you've hit the wall with your comfort zone. It lets you know you're on the path to greatness or in reaching your limit with self-doubt and ridicule. Listen to the messages and the feelings you receive. They are important clues to decipher the two. When you hear words like "you are not good enough", "you have created this mess", "you are a terrible person", those words are gremlins that are pointing you in the direction of self-love. Where can you improve your self-love in your life? Is it meditation, going for a walk, reading a book, journaling? Take time to reflect on what is really going on. Somewhere along your journey, you have taken up the act of beating yourself up as a tool to keep yourself in line. I know this gremlin too. My perfectionism taught this gremlin to keep very close tabs on me, and when I screw up, to be loud and let me know how much I suck at stuff. If you have this gremlin, you are going to talk straight to it, and you are going to free yourself from the self-loathing that has been holding you back. You created it, you can destroy it, and you, my friend, can use your superpower to do so!

Done with the self-sabotage!

Hey, you, yeah, you, the gremlin that tells me how sucky I am at living my life, yeah, I am talking to you. You forgot that I actually carry the power and that I am your creator. I have decided you don't live here anymore and it's time for you to pack your bags and move on out. Oh, and don't let the door hit you in the ass on the way out!

Now, when it happens and that fricken stinky gremlin rears its head, I want you to give it a warning that it is leaving, and you have the power to destroy it. Let it know you heard it, you now understand why it's there and what it is truly saying, and you are taking control. You have the power to turn self-loathing into self-love. It's a flick of a switch, it's a change of dialogue in your brain. It's all yours and you can do it and you are going to love yourself through it!

When you start to listen to your body and recognize what it is that you have labeled as fear, you now can start to allow it to direct you to more in your life. Yes, you read that correctly. This thing you call fear is not fearful, it's actually driving you to your dreams and desires. If you feel uneasy, that is a good thing. Your body is telling you it has never done this before and it feels "scary", but that is only because you haven't done it before. Our signals get crossed because it's the only uneasy feeling we know to connect the feeling with. Step towards it, whatever it is, putting yourself out there in a meeting, writing the song that has been rolling around in your brain, applying for the job you really want, whatever is giving you the "fear" feeling. Step towards it, then analyze what you are actually feeling which maybe "I am not good enough", "no one will like my song", I won't get the job because I am too old." Decide is that fear or is that self-doubt or something else altogether? It's time to step closer to the thing you "fear" and do something that allows momentum. Our lives work better with momentum. Once you're in motion, you can sustain motion, the hardest part is getting in motion. Take one step, then think about how you take another step, and so on.

Tap into your fears and find your greatness!

Doing the work we just described will help you find the areas in your life that need attention because our bodies are telling us so. If you tap into your "fear" and it says, "I may not get the job because I am too old", it tells you to look back at your limiting beliefs and start to pick that apart. Where did you hear that message? Do you really believe it or is it just an excuse to hold you back in the "safe zone?" Tapping into your fear is a great source for realization about what we actually think and feel. If we actually think we are too old to get the job, then guess what, you are! We are what we think. You will never even apply because you believe it to be so regardless of if it's fact or fiction. Your beliefs will guide you to making the decision not to apply. If you listen to the fear and apply anyway, then you have the opportunity to move beyond self-doubt and begin a new belief. Regardless of if you get the job or not, you have created momentum in your life to change your story.

When I started writing this book, I had many moments of self-doubt, and honestly, as I am writing right now, I wonder if many women will pick up this book and get the message as I am intending it to be, but I keep writing. I am writing for myself also. The more I write, the more I learn about myself. However, when I tell others I am writing a book, I get words of encouragement. No one has ever said, "Wow, I wonder if anyone will read it?" It's the fear or in this case, it's very strongly self-doubt and the gremlin in my head saying "you're not good enough to write a book" that pops up on a daily basis. I keep writing. It's momentum and I've welcomed my fear in, I talk to my gremlin and let it know I am going to keep writing. The more I write, the more I want to write and honestly, I am okay with whatever the outcome is. Because, at some point, the book becomes more about sitting down and letting my thoughts go free and being vulnerable enough to be courageous. My desire is to connect with others in such a way that my words may transform their lives. This is how we get to know each other. You are getting to know me and I am getting to know you. It's two women hanging out and chatting about what we fear or now as we know it, as the nudge to greatness!

It feels good to hear my fear, listen to it, identify what is really going on, and then do it anyway! I am no longer afraid to write or get it in the hands of others. It will happen if I want it to happen. If my gremlin pops its head up and says, "Hey, stop here, it sucks, no one will read it," I'll keep going, I win, not the gremlin, and guess what, if I keep doing that, I get to live my life, not a gremlin life.

Here's the thing about fear. Once you understand the language of fear, you can walk beside it and listen to it, then use it to your advantage and grow alongside it, rather than have it push you away from your dreams and desires in life. You can tame it when it's out of control, but you need to know when it's pushing you toward greatness, and when it is, go for it, sister!

66 *The braver I am,*
the luckier I get. **99**

- Glennon Doyle

Chapter Eight

Getting the momentum towards your dreams and desires.

ave you ever noticed that once you start something, it's easier to keep the momentum going? Starting small allows us to adjust our lives to add a new task or gain the courage to continue the efforts. When I change my routine or reprioritize my tasks, I start small, and it works to get the ball rolling.

Here is an exercise to get you moving:

Write down 5–10 things you can change immediately (clean out the closet, paint office, redo your flower garden). When you start small, you will notice how good it feels to have accomplished those items and it will give you the motivation to continue to make more changes. Once you have done this then write down 5–10 bigger things (writing a book, rewriting your resume, taking a class). Just act on one of them. See how it feels. Allow yourself to adjust to making these changes slowly. If I jump right into something (exercise on January 1st) without easing in, it's always a failure, but when I add walking a few times a week for 30 minutes, I eventually start jogging, eating better, adding weights. Change can be hard if we try to do it all at once and if you are like me, if it's too hard or it changes the rest of my schedule, then forget about it. It's not going to happen. Well, it happens for a week, then it's over. We want lasting change that helps move you closer to your desires. Take one thing right now and slowly add it into your to-do list or morning routine and see how it expands into your life. Another thing I noticed when I started adding things into my life slowly, was that I found some of the things I was doing daily, could actually go. They were not serving me at all. Here's an example: I used to wake up every morning around 6:00 am, make coffee, and watch the morning news. I did this for years and the funny part is that both my husband and I would watch for the weather. Then the weather would come, and we both had no idea what the weather was for the day and we'd have to check our phone app anyway! What the hell is up with that? How can you stare at the TV waiting for the weather and miss the whole damn thing? Anyway, I noticed that I used to feel informed, then it started changing my positive demeanor in the morning and I was carrying a lot on my shoulders. I realized it was just causing extra stress before I started my day. I decided that I would no longer watch the news, but I would watch the weather (small steps). That hour in the morning is now my hour to write, journal, meditate, walk, read, etc. I use the time for me, I don't give it away to the media, it's mine and my life has changed for the better because of it. Find areas in your life that are draining you versus filling you and make changes. It is amazing how much time we spend on things that do not serve us, yet say we have no time to do the things we desire. Give it a try, I bet you find a few!

" The secret of life, though, is to fall seven times and to get up eight times. "

– Paulo Coelho

Chapter Nine

Make mistakes, you learn quicker.

T hroughout your entire life, you were taught to fix your mistakes, remember the red ink on your homework assignments. I do! Those red marks would make me cringe, even if it was the "c" for correct, it still triggered me to fix something. When we are younger our parents and others who genuinely care deeply for us and were looking out for us may have used phrases such as, "Don't do it like that, you'll mess it up" or "The way you are thinking about that is all wrong." We are trained from a very early age to not listen to our instincts, to not make mistakes, and often we are told how to accomplish a goal, the way they would like to see it done. We were told how to do it. Later in life, you are afraid to make mistakes, because we see them as failures when in reality, every mistake is a lesson to move you closer to your desired outcomes. There are no mistakes, just learning moments.

I encourage you to make mistakes. The more you make, the quicker you learn and grow, and the quicker you attain the very thing you are trying to achieve. I don't believe that there are mistakes. I believe that everything we do we can learn from. So, if we learn from something, it's not a mistake, it's a process. I cannot tell you how many URLs I have purchased, branding kits I have created, business outlines I have drawn up, Facebook group or page names I have sitting on my sidebar, or websites I have started. I have had so many ideas that come to me for a business, but then as I would get into it, I'd get confused on where to start, overwhelmed with self-doubt, and afraid to screw it up, so I'd abandon them. I used to beat myself up for this, one of my gremlins would appear and tell me the reason why I was doing this. As I gained confidence in trying new things without listening to the gremlins, I noticed how much I have learned over the years about building my own business that those ideas were allowing me practice to find the right thing for me. I have grown through trial and error, and you will too, no matter what it is you desire. Allow yourself to explore ideas, concepts, techniques, and thoughts. Holding back is damming up the river. Allow the ideas to manifest and if it's not the time for them, let them go. It is okay to practice building your skills and gaining confidence in yourself. Sometimes you need to stumble for a little bit to gain confidence. Confidence doesn't come from not doing, confidence comes from doing and in some cases, all it is is trying. When we put in the effort, we learn something. Try something, learn something.

Here's the thing. Trying something and failing or changing lanes is still momentum and most people are too afraid to even try. Try and you've already gone leaps and bounds above where you were and where most will go.

When my son was in elementary and middle school, he performed on stage a lot. There were plays and performances where he skipped lines, lost his place, said lines that did not exist, etc. In the beginning, he would be very upset about this. His theater teacher would tell him that it's all part of theater and improv and as long as you keep going, nobody knows the difference. As he got older, he could recognize when his peers missed their lines and they too were improving along the way. He realized he and some of his peers were the only ones who knew his lines, so he stopped stressing out about it because if he messed up, nobody in the audience knew. They are not holding his script – and isn't that a good reminder about life?

We all mess up, it's not in the messing up that matters, it's how we proceed. In life, we get to write our own script, nobody knows if we mess it up and NOBODY cares! The only one who notices is you and the sooner you see it as a step towards your dreams, you will accept those slip-ups, failures, mistakes as practice and skill-building. Go out there and mess up. It is okay and honestly needed to advance further in your dreams.

> *"Beautiful soul… please keep being brave, when you are brave it helps me to know that I can be brave too."*

— Unknown

Chapter Ten

Your perfect formula to transform your life.

he perfect formula to transform your life is like making soup – add the parts that you like, add some parts you think will be good, add the special flavorings, and voila, you have your own unique formula to transform your life.

Oftentimes we jump into programs, challenges, internet groups, memberships, or new social groups believing that this is the fix-all. I've done it many times. I have bought countless programs that are all aimed at fixing whatever your issue is. I offer a program to women who want to convert their fear into power to transform their lives using the principles in this book. For some, a program works. For others, it's a little of this and a little of that. I gobbled up every book I could find to boil it down to the part I could use. I am inspired by books and own lots of them by different authors. My hope is that by reading the book I will get one piece of knowledge to add to my bag of tricks and tips that work for me. We are all individuals with individual needs, from our own set of circumstances, so not one solution will work for everybody. We have to be open and honest with ourselves that making the perfect soup for us takes time and it takes finding the right community or books or programs and stripping them apart to create our own perfect plan. How do you do this? Well, I am a note-taker and a highlighter and a keeper of many books. From the online programs I have bought, I write or download, if permitted, the parts I like and have a folder on my computer chock full of helpful resources. I review them at different times in my life because sometimes when something resonates with you at one time in your life, it's completely foreign at another time in your life. Have you ever picked up a book and started reading it and about two chapters in, then you put it down? It sits for months, even years, then you try it again and it's like the author is speaking directly to you? That is exactly what I mean. We are open to messages when we are ready. There is no perfect time to receive a message except for the time in which you are ready. You are on a journey and on that journey are stopping points to learn. What you absorb at different times in your life, you are building a foundation for future growth. It's okay to bounce around. There is absolutely nothing wrong with picking things up and trying them out, maybe putting them down and trying them later or discarding them completely. There is no correct way to grow. We grow as we go. We are ready when we are ready. Life is not a race; you are on your unique path to personal, professional and spiritual growth. Take time to smell the roses, jump the rocks in the river, listen to songs that remind you of another time in your life, bake delicious pastries. Whatever turns you on at the time, is exactly what you should be doing, and it is a huge part of trusting yourself through the process.

Establishing a morning routine.

Do you have a morning routine? I would highly recommend getting into one. I never did until I became sober. Heck, when I was drinking wine, mornings were something I did not want to see, let alone get up before the sun to write, meditate, read, or exercise. Now, I long for it. I go to bed ready to rest and wake up refreshed (by the way, I have a cat who does not agree with my plan and likes to keep me up all night. Any tips on that, I'll take them!)

When you get up early, you begin your day with a fresh set of eyes. Now, I know many of you that are more productive in the evening. If that's you, that's great. Just create an evening routine. Whenever you feel energized, get into a routine and flow with it. I love mornings because my house is quiet, I can focus, and I love coffee. Coffee is actually a motivator for getting out of bed and starting my morning routine. I have a pact though, that I don't start coffee until 5:30 a.m. Sometimes I am up at 4:30 a.m. because I honestly love my mornings. I plan my day, write, read, and meditate. I have more focus and my best ideas come in the morning. Before I go to bed, I visualize my morning. When I wake up, I'm ready to slay! And, for this book, it's the time that I just write. I wake up and get into the flow and allow the words to stream through me onto paper, feeling it word by word. I visualize that you and others are reading this book and getting some helpful information that will transform fear into power to transform your life.

Make tiny upgrades that greatly impact your confidence.

To make a change in your life, it's okay to start very small with something you can upgrade. I love this because when you make a small change, it feels like you have moved mountains.

Denise Duffield-Thomas, author of *Get Rich, Lucky Bitch*, writes about making changes that you can start right away to give you confidence and upgrade where you can. I read her book and started looking around my house to see where I could make small changes that translated to big upgrades in my world. I really wanted to paint our office. It's actually a dining room, but it's too small to put a table and chairs comfortably in it, so it has become our office. All of the interior walls in our house when we moved in were white. Good base, I suppose, but it gets dirty and when raising a child and having dogs, you get the picture. It's hard to keep clean. Anyway, I wanted to paint the office a grey color, but because it would require a lot of fixing to the walls, I settled on two walls. Okay, two walls, no big deal. Heck yeah. Months went by, a color was picked, months went by, another color, ugh. At this point, I'm ready to paint it with whatever leftover paint we have in the basement. I didn't care, let's just paint the walls. However, my motivation was to find an upgrade. I am so sick of seeing tack holes, half-peeled-off stickers from when my son was a toddler, and dog claw marks from years ago. I need a damn upgrade. Well, I got it! And can I just tell you that the small upgrade of two walls painted grey, feels like a Ferrari in my driveway? You wouldn't actually want to park a Ferrari in my driveway as it's dirt with potholes currently, but you get what I'm saying. Now, what does this have to do with anything? Well, as Denise explains in her book, the tiny little upgrade will get you into motion and it gives you a sense of pride in your own environment. That was huge for me! I bought a few house plants, and I got a throw rug. None of this was pricey, just feels good to upgrade a tiny bit. By doing things you can do, tiny upgrades, you upgrade your life. You show yourself that you and your home and your family are worthy of the upgrade.

Want to try it? Start with your closet. I buy second-hand clothes all the time. I'm okay with that because I like keeping clothes from ending up in landfills, especially if they are my size and I love them! But sometimes my closet gets overpacked with stuff I don't wear. There are a lot of clothes I never wear, but I liked the color or at one time it spoke to me, or a friend offered it to me, and I added it to my closet. But, if you don't wear it, ditch it. It's okay. When your closet reflects how you feel now and what to look at today, you will wear it more confidently and you will be offering someone else an opportunity for a great find. Recycle them, let someone else feel the excitement of finding the perfect outfit, and filling their closet with items that represent who they are today (not 10 years ago), it's really okay to let go of the sweater gifted to you by your aunt that you never wore. It's okay, someone really wants that sweater and by removing it, you've made peace with the fact that every time you see it, you feel guilty for not wearing it for an auntie. I've got shit like that too and it doesn't help that I am extremely sentimental. I attach so much meaning to stuff that getting rid of something a family member or friend gave me, especially if they have passed, is an issue, but I do it because I know someone else is longing for that thing. Ultimately, it's only a material possession that has no real value, only the value we place on it. If you don't resonate with it, it's draining from your positive energy. So, start small. Denise suggests making a list of ideas of places you can clear out or upgrade, even slightly, then take action. You'll feel amazing after.

Add the happy.

Mix some journaling, meditation, breathing exercises, walking, nature, whatever it is that makes you happy and instills routine into your day. By doing this, you are not only trying new things to see what sticks, but you're making small changes that are signaling to your brain something new, something different is happening. It's amazing how quickly you start to feel creative, empowered, and ready to make a change.

Get on your to-do list.

Add yourself to your to-do list as soon as possible or get yourself on your calendar. This is so important and so overlooked because we are so used to getting the scraps, whatever is leftover. Not anymore. You are the priority. You must make time for yourself to journal, meditate, write, read, go for a walk, etc. I physically schedule my breaks in my calendar now because I won't take them otherwise and then I'll complain how tired and unappreciated I feel when I am the one creating the schedule. I feel unappreciated because I treat myself that way. When we treat ourselves as not being important, we signal to the world that we feel we are unimportant. We must schedule ourselves in. We must take better care of ourselves so that we can be fully present for others.

No more sweating the small stuff.

Let's not sweat the small stuff, anymore! It's time to move on and focus your limited daily energy on positive change and things that fuel your positive energy, not deplete it. You only have so much energy allotted per day. When you stress over crap that never turns up, you waste so much precious energy. Worse still, you waste your capacity to build more of what you want in your life. It's time to let shit go and focus on what you can do, not the crap that you have no control over. What's done is done, you have control over the present, that's it. What you do now shows up in your future, so choose wisely because tomorrow is coming!

Muck it up, it's mandatory!

The best lesson I have learned about change is to go out and try new things and make some mistakes, it's okay – no, it's a must-do! When you try new things, your body naturally resists them. It's natural and completely normal to resist change or a new activity. Your brain has no idea what is happening, so it goes into default mode and resists it. No, thank you! Sometimes when I try new things, I create bullshit stories about how bad something is going to turn out or how I cannot do it. I limit myself before I even try. The trick here is to convince your brain that you're looking to make a mistake, so you can experience the new thing. Tell your brain, "It's okay, I'm hoping I make a mistake, so I can do it better next time. No pressure, just you and me, and most likely a mistake, so we got this!" Tell yourself that the mistake is the goal, then your brain shifts into "Okay, let's try it" mode. If you can get your brain into "let's try it" mode, then the next time you do it, it's not the first time. It will never be the first time again. It allows your brain to make connections and chalk it up to "oh yeah, we did this before, I know what to do" mode. That's where the good stuff starts. Just move past the first step and take the leap. Mel Robbins, the author of *The 5 Second Rule*, shows people how to make a change in 5 seconds by counting backward and doing it, whatever it is. Once you do it once, you're golden. You either add it to your list of ingredients to your soup or you move on, but at least you know how you feel about it.

Oh, and finally, thank you, fear – I'll take it from here!

If nothing else, listen to your fear – discern if it's a nudge to greatness (if so, embrace the nudge) or outside of your values (nod it off). This is the key to overcoming self-doubt. Walk with your fears, don't push them away. Hold your fear's hand. Talk with it. Get to know exactly what it is whispering to you. The more you fight or push it off, the more it will show up. Fear is powerful, in the sense that it is your inner voice, but don't give it power if it's pushing you away. Embrace the shit in your life, understand that the power we give it, it has. That is it! You give it no power, it has none. You give it power; it has a hold on you. You decide. How much power are you giving fear rather than dealing with it? Real fear – the fear of being hit by a car, the fear of falling off a cliff, the fear of being chased by a dog with his teeth showing – is different from the fear of failure. The fear of being in imminent danger tells you to move, or you will be in pain. But, when we label every uncomfortable feeling with fear, we limit ourselves tremendously. We create our fear, by deciding we are afraid. When you begin to use the word fear as an all-encompassing word that really translates into "I don't want to do this", "I have never done this before", "I am nervous", "I am uneasy", you just gave one word that has so much impact on how you perceive the feeling a lot of power over you and your actions. Fear is something to listen to, not run from. It is the language nudging you toward greatness that you translate in your own way. Rephrasing I am not good enough to I am beyond good enough, is the power of goddesses. Just the simple reword will empower you and drive you toward your dreams.

Your soup is only for you.

Trust that only you can make your soup, your way, with your own ingredients. Allow yourself to experiment, but never, ever, disregard putting in something that you've never tasted before. That may be the one ingredient that will shift your entire life. Mix it up, change, when necessary, most of all forgive yourself when shit doesn't work out as you had planned. Life is a dance, and you get to dance every day if you allow yourselves the opportunity. Don't take yourself so seriously and watch how your life is transformed.

The universe buries strange jewels deep within us all, and then stands back to see if we can find them.

– Elizabeth Gilbert

Chapter Eleven
You are exactly where you are supposed to be.

e want certainty, we want to feel content, we want the outcome to be here now, but it is in the process that we truly find ourselves. The universe unfolds for us when we are ready. Opportunities show up when we believe that we are worthy of them. You are exactly where you are supposed to be right now at this very moment. The experiences in your life are not by accident. We are meant to learn in this life, not just sit stagnant. Our experiences shape us, mold us, stretch us into the amazing souls we are today. Keep your eyes open, ears alert, and face to the sun. Everything you are and are becoming is beautiful. We love looking at the butterfly when her wings are spread, and never question her creation in her cocoon. There is beauty in our unfolding. Our personal growth is a process, and while we are growing, we are transforming from the inside out.

You, my friend, are divine so shine, shine, shine!

You may not know this or understand how powerful you are. I get it, I was there once too. Here's a secret, you are a part of the universe, and you are made up of energy. Yeah, that's mind-blowing, isn't it? I remember hearing it for the first time back at Mike Dooley's conference in Boston in 2013. Holy crap, I thought, I am divine and then I started looking around the room and saw all the other divine souls with me. We are not just here to wander aimlessly around this planet, we are meant to thrive. You are meant to thrive. Dr. Wayne Dyer has a wonderful quote "See the light in others and treat them as if that is all that you see." I encourage you to see the light in yourself as well and understand that you are far more than you allow yourself to believe you are. Step into your light, shine bright, let others feel your bright light and energy. Only in the light, can you move into full self-love and trust. When you are there, you will know and feel that you have everything you need in this life, already inside of you. Embrace the higher self that is nudging you toward greatness and walk among those who choose to see the same and use your light to move those who are not yet enlightened to the truths of their own greatness. You, my friend, are divine, so shine, shine, shine!

With massive love,

Mandy

References.

1. Merriam-Webster, s.v. "consciousness," accessed June 19, 2021, https://www.meriam-webster.com/dictionary/conciousness.

2. "Subconscious vs. Unconscious: What's the difference?," *Writing Explained*, accessed June 19, 2021, https://www.writingexplained.org/subconscious-vs-unconscious-difference.

3. Scott Jeffrey, "Repressed Emotions: A Guide to Understanding Feelings Hidden Within Us (And How to Transmute Them)," last accessed June 19, 2021, https://scottjeffrey.com/repressed-emotions/.

4. A.J. Adams, "Seeing Is Believing: The Power of Visualization," *Psychology Today*, last modified December 3, 2009, https://www.psychologytoday.com/us/blog/flourish/200912/seeing-is-believing-the-power-visualization.

Made in the USA
Middletown, DE
05 September 2021